CHORDS & SCALES
IN THE BEGINNING
CREATED ESPECIALLY FOR BASSISTS

BY MAX PALERMO

A practical approach for playing scales over any chord progression to strengthen your bass lines, groove patterns and solo ideas.
For 4 & 5 strings.

ISBN-13: 978-1-57424-224-9
ISBN-10: 1-57424-224-5
SAN-683-8022

Copyright © 2007 CENTERSTREAM Publishing, LLC
P.O. Box 17878 - Anaheim Hills, CA 92817

Contents

Introduction

The aim of this book is to provide the bass player with a practical reference guide through the different scale choices that may be applied to the most commonly used types of chords.

A clear image of this topic makes it possible to choose the right and proper sounds to play and improvise over any chord progressions. You will discover countless combinations to create more interesting melodies and to enrich your grooves with new and diverse patterns in every given musical situation.

For each chord in this book you will find the relevant scale summaries presented in the same key (C), to allow you to pick out the similarities and differences. The chords in relation listed at the bottom are the other chords of the same family for which the scale is suitable.

I would advise you to play these scales chromatically up the fretboard, transposing them into all the keys, and to concentrate on the notes you are playing, possibly singing them with your voice so as to memorize their sound.

I'm sure you will find this practice greatly beneficial for handling bass lines and performing solos in any key.

Enjoy your work!

Relationships

major scale

lydian mode

major pentatonic scale

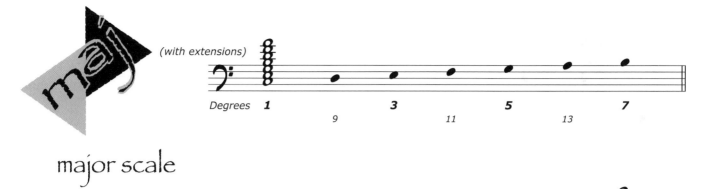

Degrees **1** **3** **5** **7**

9 11 13

major scale

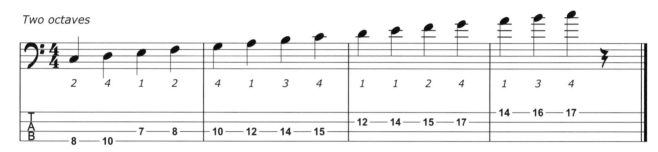

Fingers 2 4 | 1 2 | 4 1 | 3 4

Two octaves

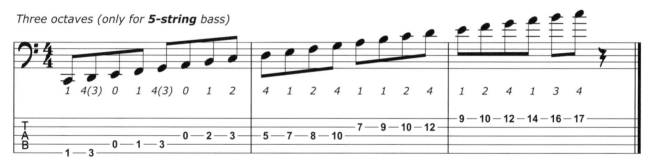

2 4 1 2 | 4 1 3 4 | 1 1 2 4 | 1 3 4

*Three octaves (only for **5-string** bass)*

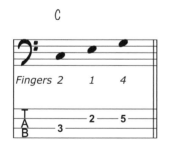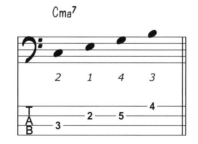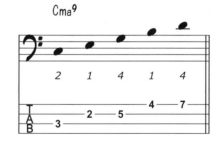

1 4(3) 0 1 4(3) 0 1 2 | 4 1 2 4 1 1 2 4 | 1 2 4 1 3 4

Chords in relation

C

Fingers 2 1 4

Cma⁷

2 1 4 3

Cma⁹

2 1 4 1 4

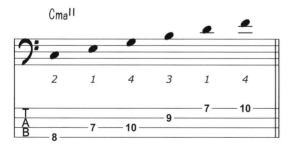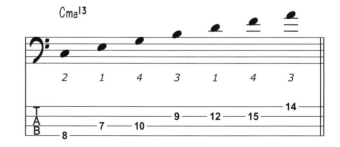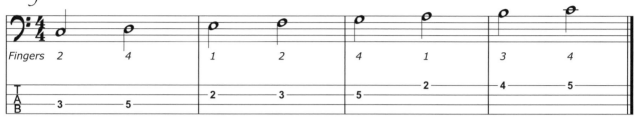

Cma¹¹

2 1 4 3 1 4

Cma¹³

2 1 4 3 1 4 3

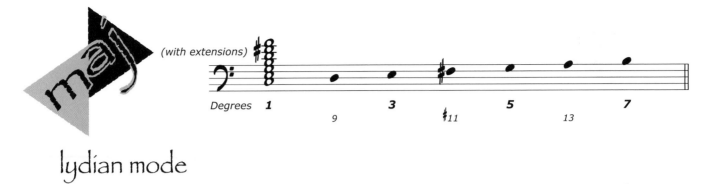

Degrees **1** **3** **5** **7**

9 #11 13

lydian mode

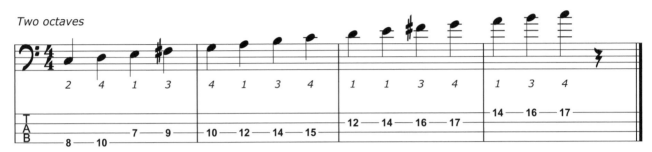

Fingers 2 4 1 3 4 1 3 4

Two octaves

2 4 1 3 4 1 3 4 1 1 3 4 1 3 4

*Three octaves (only for **5-string** bass)*

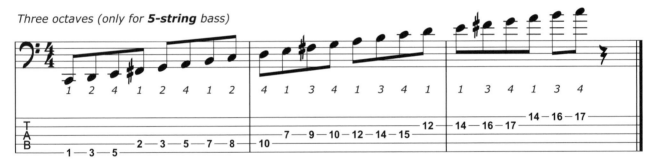

1 2 4 1 2 4 1 2 4 1 3 4 1 3 4 1 1 3 4 1 3 4

Chords in relation

C

Fingers 2 1 4

Cma⁷

2 1 4 3

Cma⁹

2 1 4 1 4

Cma⁹⁽♯¹¹⁾

2 1 4 3 1 4

Cma¹³⁽♯¹¹⁾

2 1 4 3 1 1 4

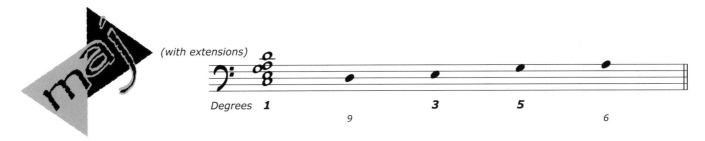

(with extensions)

Degrees **1** **3** **5** **6**

9

major pentatonic scale

Fingers 2 4 1 4 1 4

Two octaves

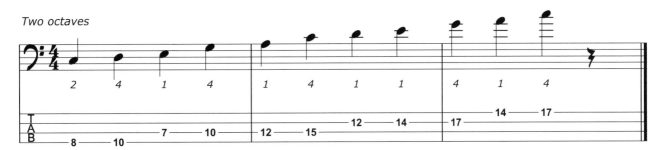

2 4 1 4 1 4 1 1 4 1 4

*Three octaves (only for **5-string** bass)*

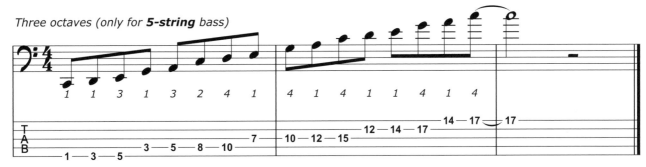

1 1 3 1 3 2 4 1 4 1 4 1 1 4 1 4

Chords in relation

C C^6 Cma^7

Fingers 2 1 4

$C^{(add\ 9)}$ $C^{6/9}$

dorian mode

1   2   b3   4   5   6   b7   8

phrygian mode

1   b2   b3   4   5   b6   b7   8

natural minor scale

1   2   b3   4   5   b6   b7   8

melodic minor scale

1   2   b3   4   5   6   7   8

harmonic minor scale

1   2   b3   4   5   b6   7   8

blues scale

1   b3   4   #4   5   b7   8

minor pentatonic scale

1   b3   4   5   b7   8

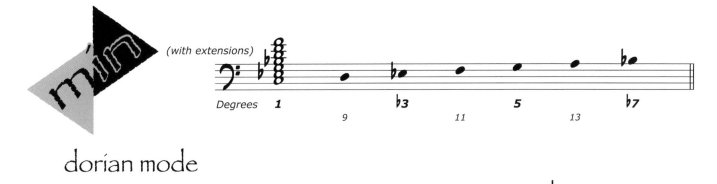

(with extensions)

Degrees **1**   ♭**3**   **5**   ♭**7**

9   11   13

dorian mode

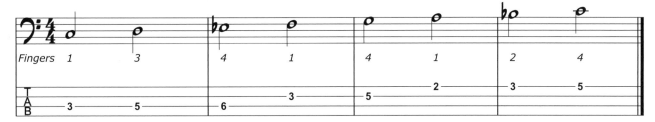

Fingers   1   3   4   1   4   1   2   4

Two octaves

*Three octaves (only for **5-string** bass)*

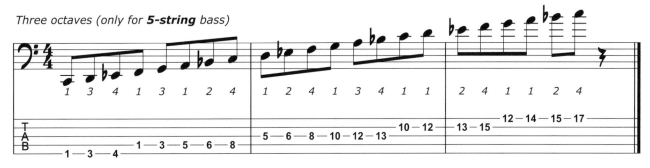

Chords in relation

Cm

Fingers 1   4   3

Cm⁷

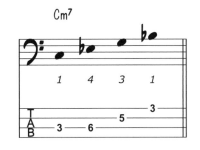

Cm⁹

Cm¹¹

Cm¹³

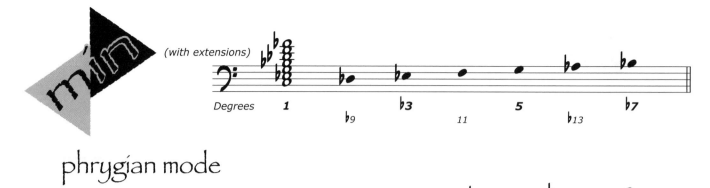

Degrees   **1**   b9   **b3**   11   **5**   b13   **b7**

phrygian mode

Two octaves

*Three octaves (only for **5-string** bass)*

Chords in relation

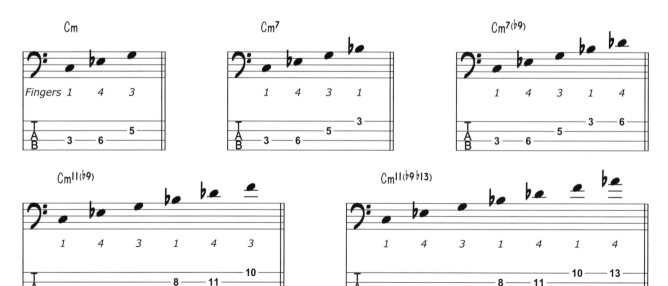

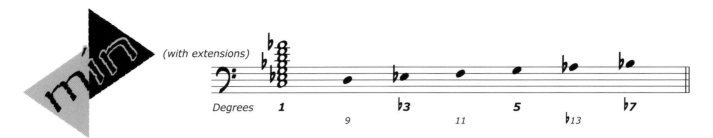

(with extensions)

Degrees   **1**   9   **♭3**   11   **5**   ♭13   **♭7**

natural minor scale

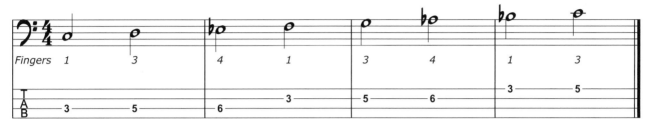

Two octaves

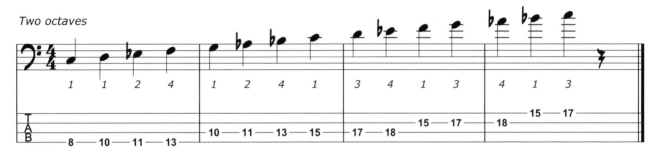

*Three octaves (only for **5-string** bass)*

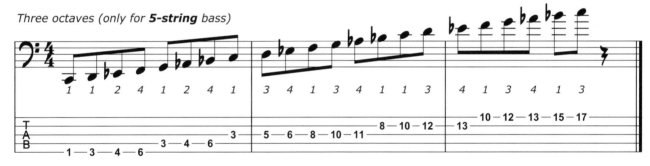

Chords in relation

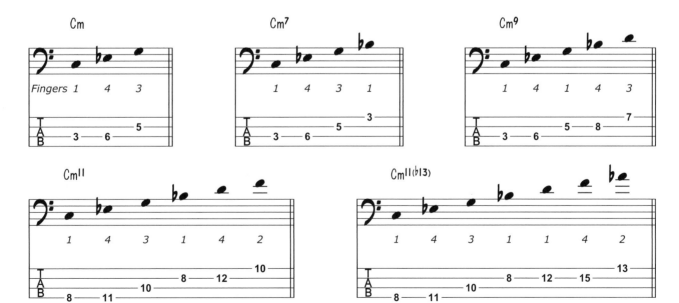

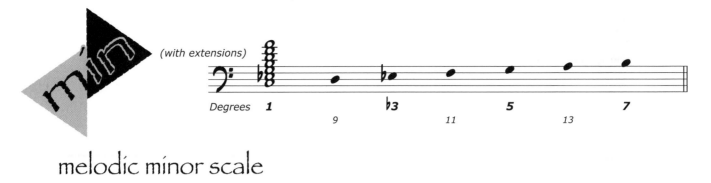

(with extensions)

Degrees   **1**   **♭3**   **5**   **7**

9   11   13

melodic minor scale

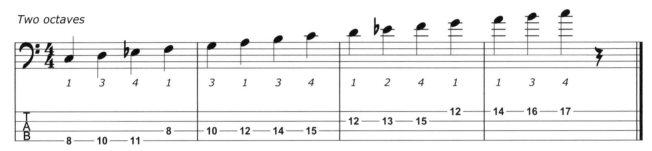

Two octaves

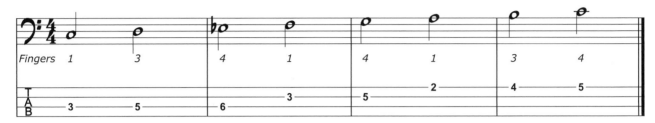

*Three octaves (only for **5-string** bass)*

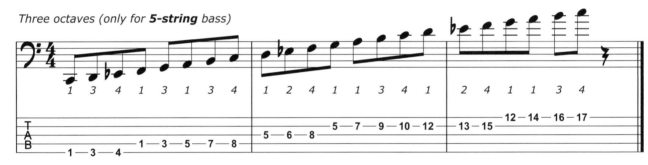

Chords in relation

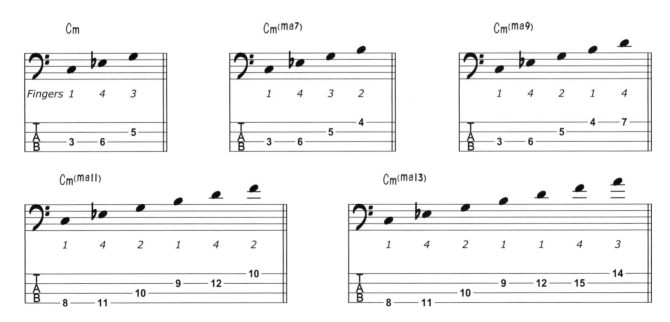

Cm   Cm(ma7)   Cm(ma9)

Cm(ma11)   Cm(ma13)

(with extensions)

Degrees **1**   9   **♭3**   **11**   **5**   **♭13**   **7**

harmonic minor scale

Fingers   1   3   4   1   3   4   2   3

Two octaves

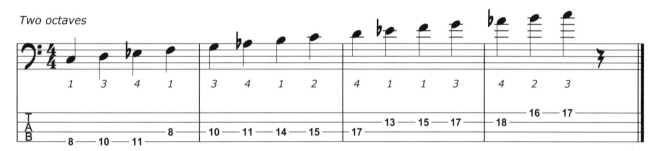

*Three octaves (only for **5-string** bass)*

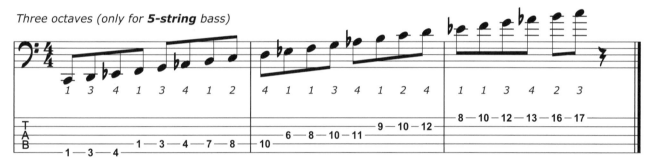

Chords in relation

Cm   Cm(ma7)   Cm(ma9)

Cm(ma11)   Cm(ma11♭13)

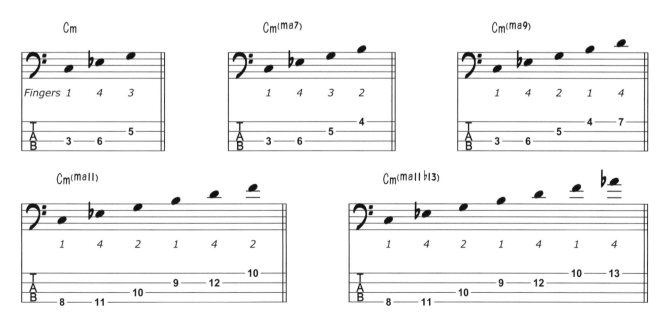

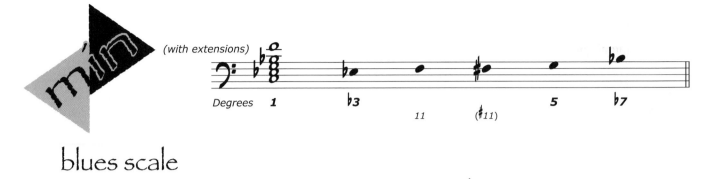

(with extensions)

Degrees   **1**   **♭3**   *11*   *(♯11)*   **5**   **♭7**

blues scale

Fingers   1   4   1   2   3   1   3

Two octaves

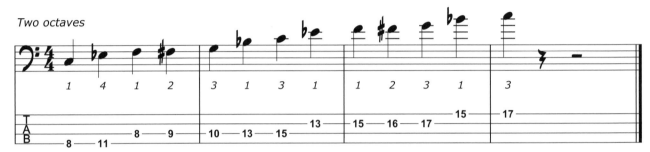

1   4   1   2   3   1   3   1   1   2   3   1   3

*Three octaves (only for **5-string** bass)*

1   4   1   2   3   1   3   1   1   2   3   1   3   1   1   2   3   1   3

Chords in relation

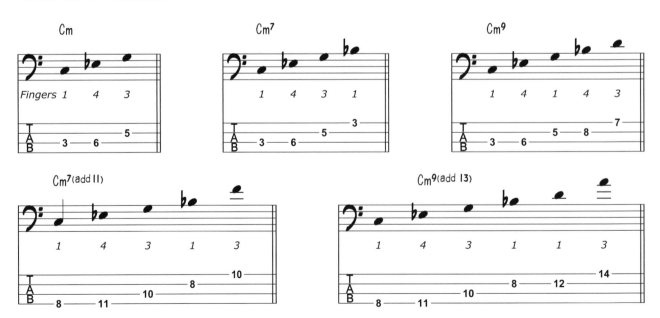

Cm

Fingers 1   4   3

Cm⁷

1   4   3   1

Cm⁹

1   4   1   4   3

Cm⁷(add 11)

1   4   3   1   3

Cm⁹(add 13)

1   4   3   1   1   3

(with extensions)

Degrees   **1**   **♭3**   **5**   **♭7**

11

minor pentatonic scale

Two octaves

Three octaves (only for **5-string** bass)

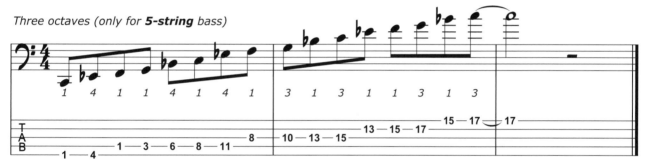

Chords in relation

Cm

Cm⁷

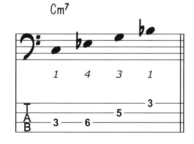

Cm⁹

Cm¹¹

Cm¹³

dim ———— Chord/Scale

Relationships

diminished scale

1   2   b3   4   b5   b6   bb7   ♮7   8

altered ^{bb7} mode

1   b2   b3   b4   b5   b6   bb7   8

harmonic major – mode 7

1   b2   b3   4   b5   b6   bb7   8

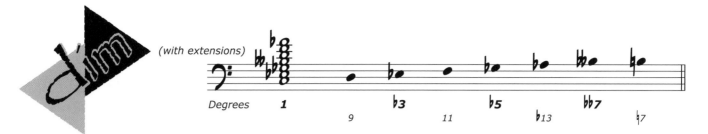

(with extensions)

Degrees **1**   9   **b3**   11   **b5**   **b13**   **bb7**   **♮7**

diminished scale

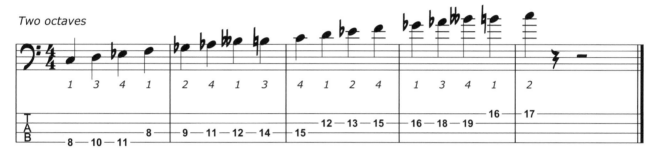

Fingers   1   3   4   1   1   3   4   1   2

Two octaves

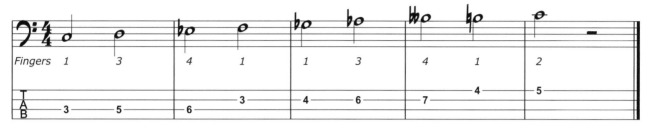

*Three octaves (only for **5-string** bass)*

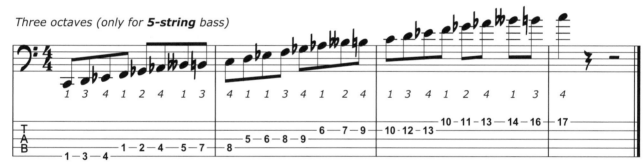

Chords in relation

C°   C°7   C°7(add ma7)

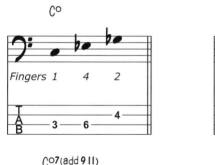  

Fingers 1   4   2

C°7(add 9 11)   C°7(add 9 11 b13)

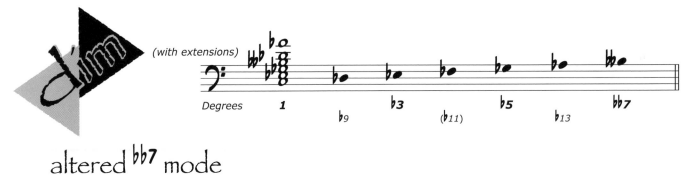

dim *(with extensions)*

Degrees	**1**		**b3**		**b5**		**bb7**
		b9		(b11)		b13	

altered ᵇᵇ⁷ mode

| Fingers | 1 | 1 | 3 | 4 | 1 | 3 | 4 | 2 |

Two octaves

*Three octaves (only for **5-string** bass)*

Chords in relation

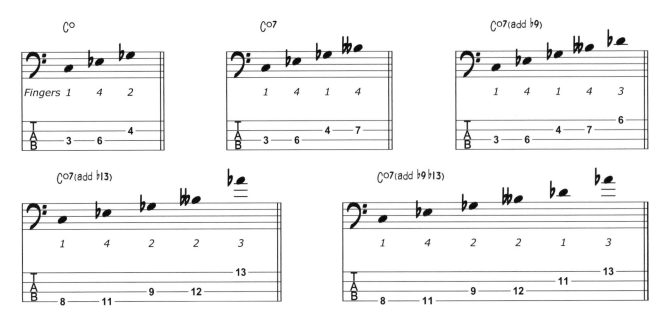

C°

C°7

C°7(add b9)

C°7(add b13)

C°7(add b9 b13)

(with extensions)

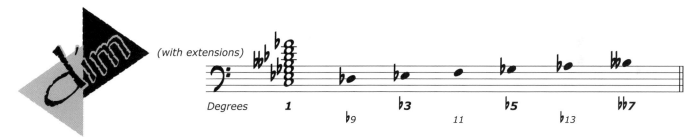

Degrees   **1**   ♭9   **♭3**   11   **♭5**   ♭13   **♭♭7**

harmonic major ~ mode 7

Two octaves

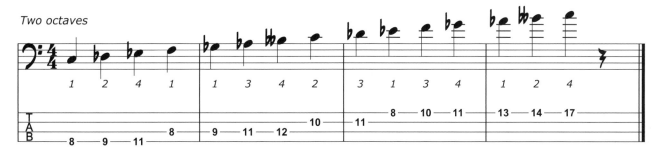

Three octaves (only for 5-string bass)

Chords in relation

C°

C°7

C°7(add ♭9)

C°7(add ♭9 11)

C°7(add ♭9 11 ♭13)

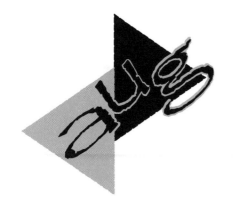

Relationships

augmented scale

1   #2   3   5   #5   7   8

lydian augmented mode

1   2   3   #4   #5   6   7   8

ionian #5 mode

1   2   3   4   #5   6   7   8

(with extensions)

Degrees   **1**   ♯9   **3**   **(5)**   ♯**5**   **7**

augmented scale

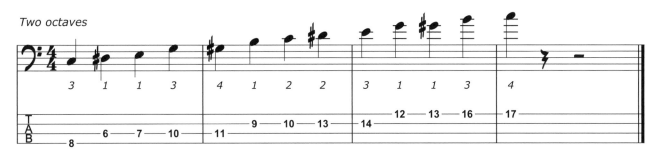

Two octaves

*Three octaves (only for **5-string** bass)*

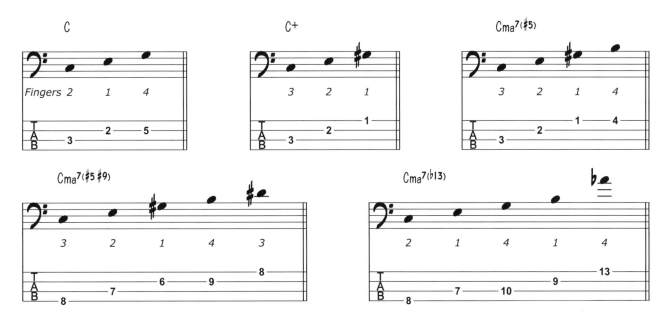

Chords in relation

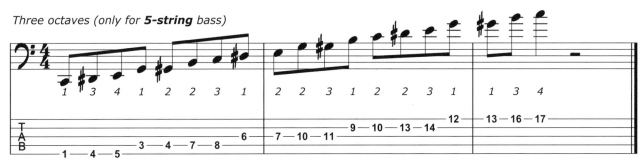

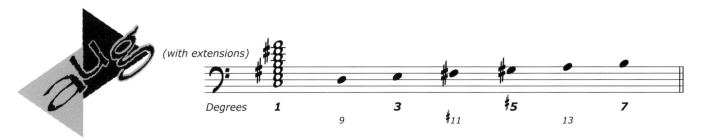

aug (with extensions)

Degrees   **1**   **3**   ♯**5**   **7**
               9   ♯11   13

lydian augmented mode

Fingers   2   4   1   1   3   4   1   2

Two octaves

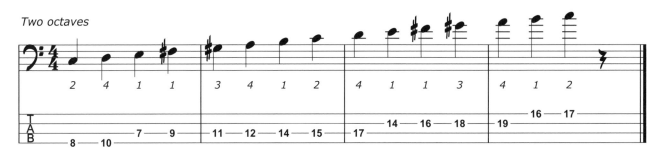

2 4 1 1 3 4 1 2 4 1 1 3 4 1 2

*Three octaves (only for **5-string** bass)*

1 2 4 1 3 4 1 2 4 1 1 3 4 1 2 4 1 1 3 4 1 2

Chords in relation

C+

Fingers 3   2   1

Cma⁷(♯5)

3   2   1   4

Cma⁹(♯5)

3   2   1   1   4

Cma⁹(♯5♯11)

3   2   1   1   4   3

Cma¹³(♯5♯11)

2   1   1   4   2   1   4

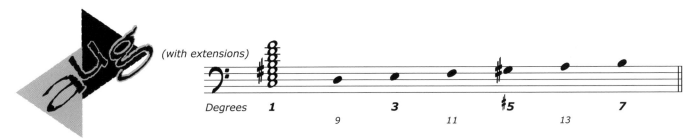

(with extensions)

Degrees **1** **3** **♯5** **7**

9   11   13

Ionian ♯5 mode

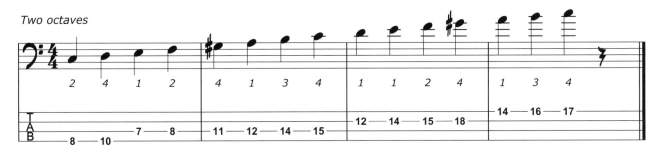

Fingers 2   4   1   2   1   1   3   4

Two octaves

2 4 1 2   4 1 3 4   1 1 2 4   1 3 4

Three octaves (only for **5-string** bass)

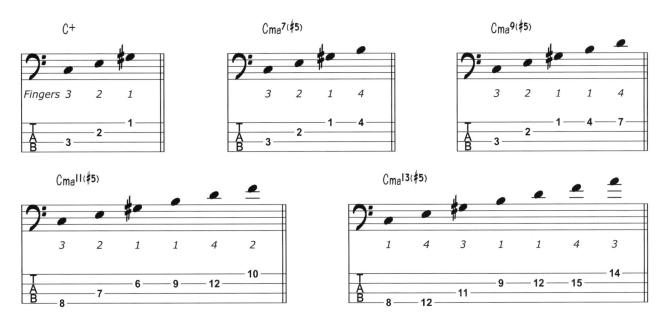

1 3 0 1 4 1 3 4   1 1 2 4 1 3 4 1   1 2 4 1 3 4

Chords in relation

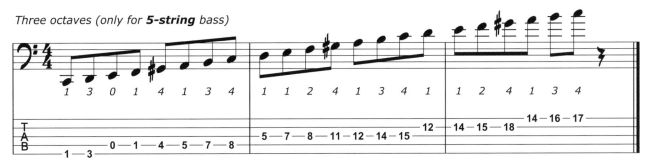

C+

Fingers 3   2   1

Cma⁷(♯5)

3   2   1   4

Cma⁹(♯5)

3   2   1   1   4

Cma¹¹(♯5)

3   2   1   1   4   2

Cma¹³(♯5)

1   4   3   1   1   4   3

major scale (no3)

1   2   4   5   6   7   8

mixolydian mode (no3)

1   2   4   5   6   ♭7   8

major pentatonic - mode 2

1   2   4   5   ♭7   8

major pentatonic - mode 4

1   2   4   5   6   8

kumoi pentatonic - mode 2

1   ♭2   4   5   ♭7   8

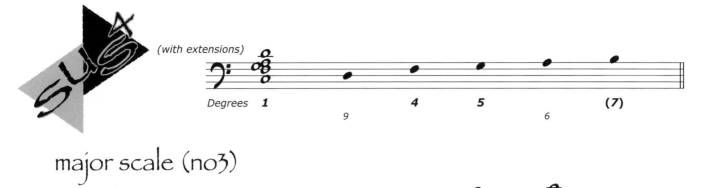

(with extensions)

Degrees **1** **4** **5** **(7)**

9 6

major scale (no3)

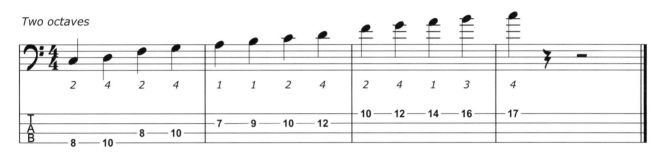

Fingers 2 4 | 2 4 | 1 3 | 4

Two octaves

2 4 2 4 | 1 1 2 4 | 2 4 1 3 | 4

Three octaves (only for **5-string** bass)

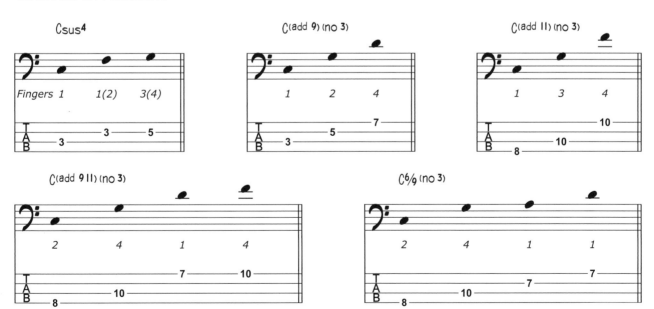

1 3 1 3 1 3 4 1 | 1(2) 4 1 1 2 4 2 4 | 1 3 4

Chords in relation

Csus**4**

Fingers 1 1(2) 3(4)

C(add **9**) (no 3)

1 2 4

C(add 11) (no 3)

1 3 4

C(add **9** 11) (no 3)

2 4 1 4

C**6/9** (no 3)

2 4 1 1

~ 25 ~

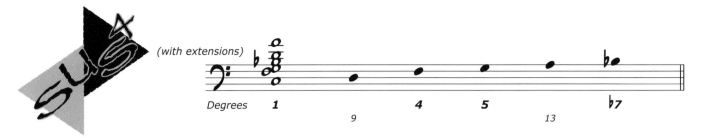

(with extensions)

Degrees **1** 　 　 **4** 　 **5** 　 　 **♭7**

9 　 　 　 13

mixolydian mode (no3)

Fingers 　2 　 　 4 　 　 2 　 　 4 　 　 1 　 　 2 　 　 4

Two octaves

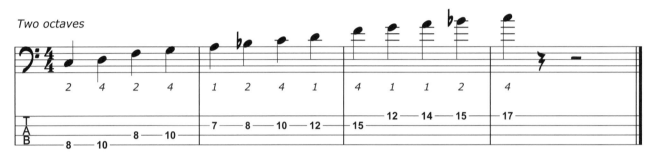

2 　 4 　 2 　 4 　 1 　 2 　 4 　 1 　 4 　 1 　 1 　 2 　 4

*Three octaves (only for **5-string** bass)*

1 　3 　1 　3 　1 　2 　4 　1 　1(2) 　4 　1 　2 　4 　1 　4 　1 　1 　2 　4

Chords in relation

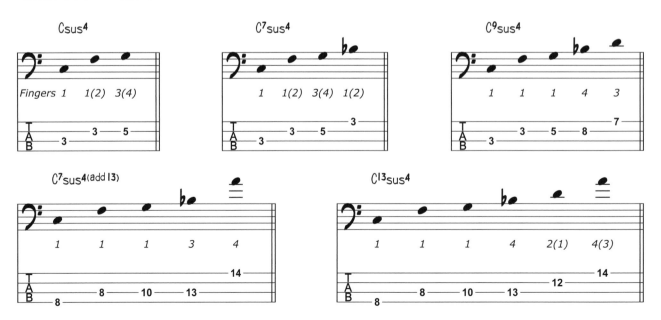

Csus⁴

Fingers 1 　1(2) 　3(4)

C⁷sus⁴

1 　1(2) 　3(4) 　1(2)

C⁹sus⁴

1 　1 　1 　4 　3

C⁷sus⁴(add 13)

1 　1 　1 　3 　4

C¹³sus⁴

1 　1 　1 　4 　2(1) 　4(3)

Degrees   **1**   **4**   **5**   **♭7**

9

major pentatonic ~ mode 2

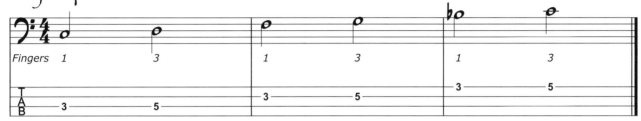

Fingers   1   3   1   3   1   3

Two octaves

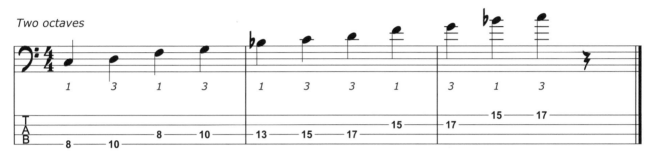

*Three octaves (only for **5-string** bass)*

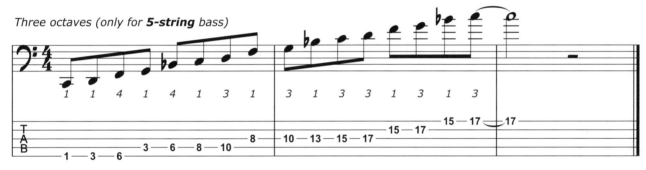

Chords in relation

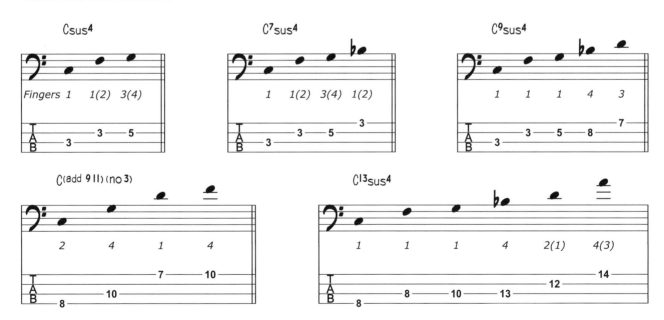

C_{sus}⁴   C⁷_{sus}⁴   C⁹_{sus}⁴

C(add 9 11) (no 3)   C¹³_{sus}⁴

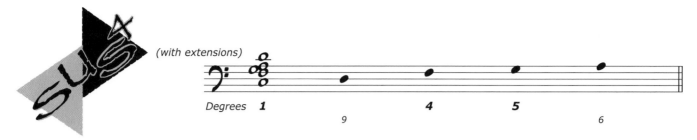

(with extensions)

Degrees   **1**   9   **4**   **5**   6

major pentatonic - mode 4

Two octaves

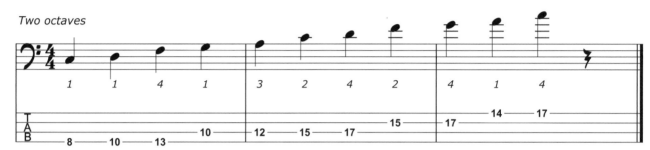

*Three octaves (only for **5-string** bass)*

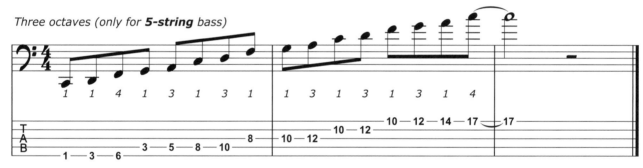

Chords in relation

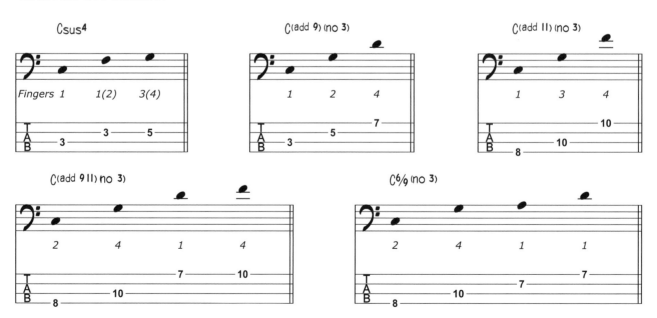

Csus⁴   C(add 9) (no 3)   C(add 11) (no 3)

C(add 9 11) (no 3)   C6/9 (no 3)

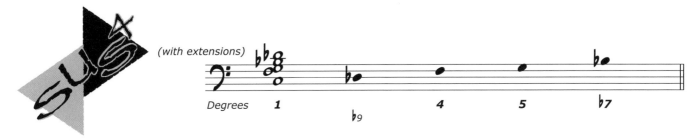

(with extensions)

Degrees **1** **4** **5** **♭7**

♭9

kumoí pentatoníc ~ mode 2

Fingers 1   2   1   3   1   3

Two octaves

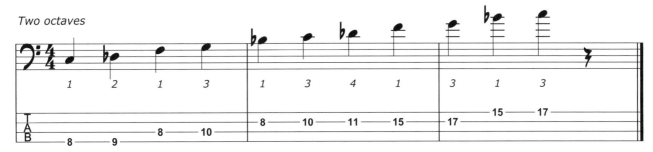

Three octaves (only for 5-string bass)

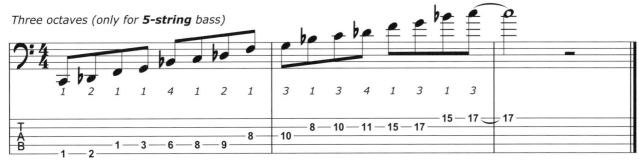

Chords in relation

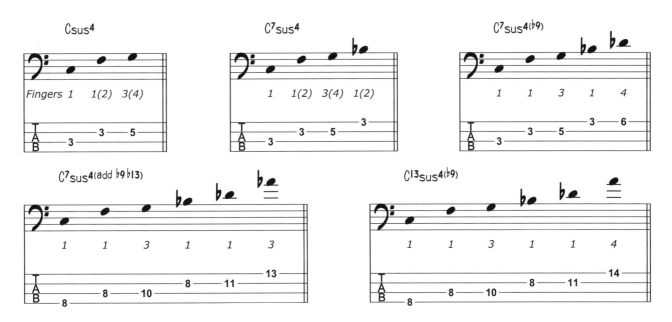

C sus4

C7sus4

C7sus4(♭9)

C7sus4(add ♭9 ♭13)

C13sus4(♭9)

Relationships

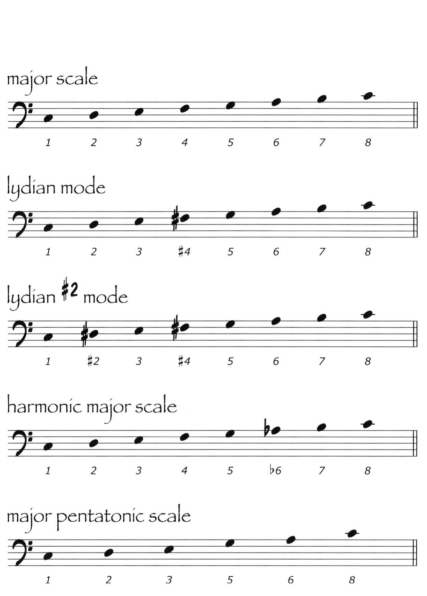

major scale

1 2 3 4 5 6 7 8

lydian mode

1 2 3 #4 5 6 7 8

lydian #2 mode

1 #2 3 #4 5 6 7 8

harmonic major scale

1 2 3 4 5 ♭6 7 8

major pentatonic scale

1 2 3 5 6 8

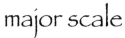 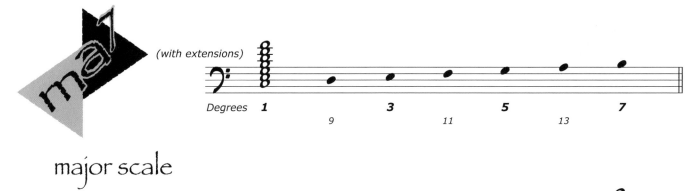

(with extensions)

Degrees **1**   **3**   **5**   **7**

            9   *11*   *13*

major scale

Two octaves

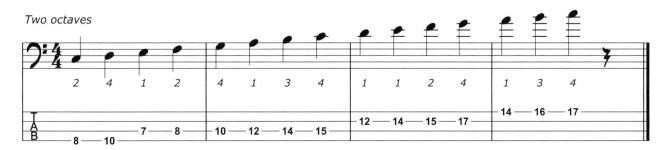

*Three octaves (only for **5-string** bass)*

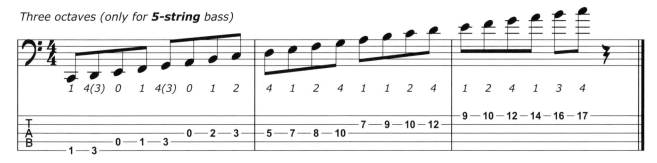

Chords in relation

C   Cma⁷   Cma⁹

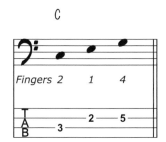 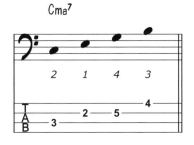 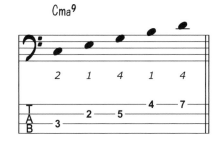

Cma¹¹   Cma¹³

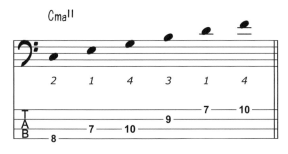 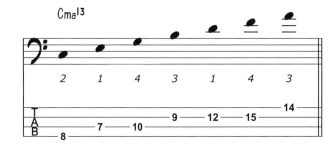

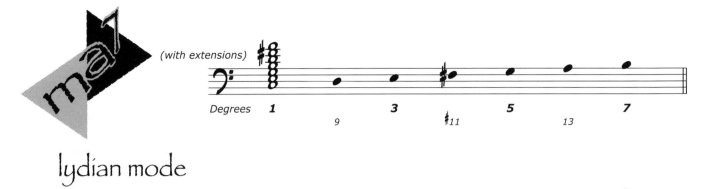

Degrees **1** **3** **5** **7**
9 ♯11 13

lydian mode

Fingers 2   4   1   3   4   1   3   4

Two octaves

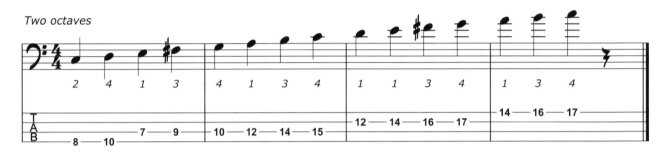

*Three octaves (only for **5-string** bass)*

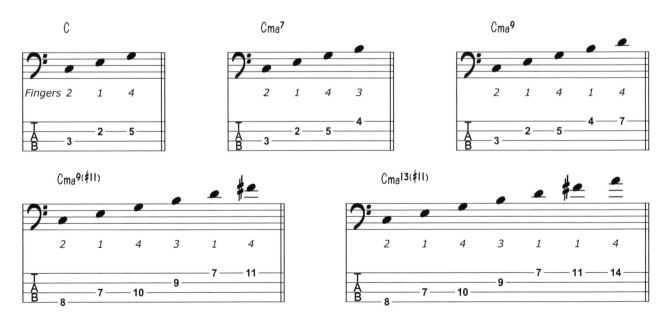

Chords in relation

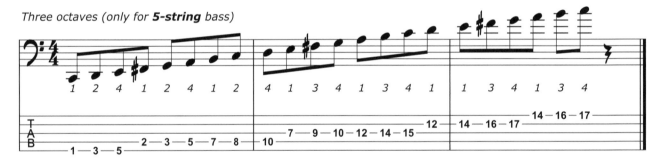

(with extensions)

Degrees **1** **3** **5** **7**

$\sharp 9$ $\sharp 11$ 13

lydian $\sharp 2$ mode

Fingers 3 1 1 3 4 1 3 4

Two octaves

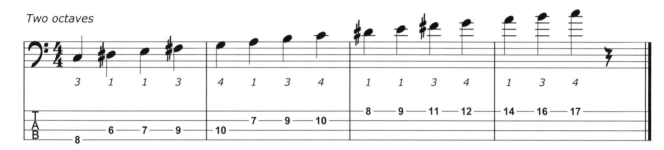

3 1 1 3 4 1 3 4 1 1 3 4 1 3 4

Three octaves (only for 5-string bass)

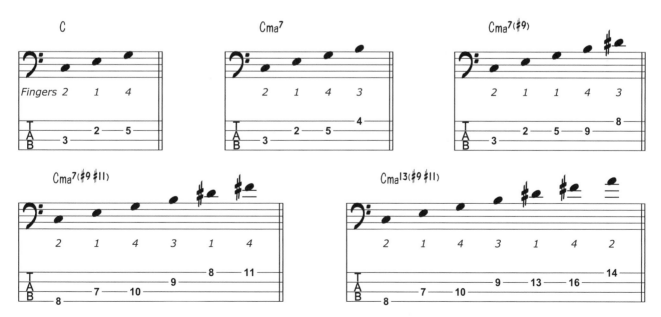

1 3 4 1 2 4 1 2 4 1 3 4 1 3 4 1 1 3 4 1 3 4

Chords in relation

C Cma7 Cma7(♯9)

Fingers 2 1 4 2 1 4 3 2 1 1 4 3

Cma7(♯9 ♯11) Cma13(♯9 ♯11)

2 1 4 3 1 4 2 1 4 3 1 4 2

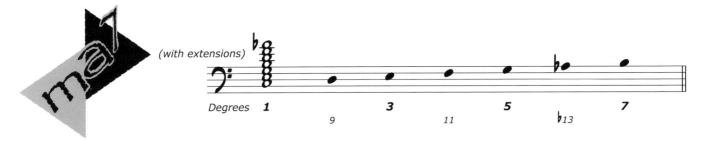

Degrees **1** 9   **3** 11   **5** ♭13   **7**

harmonic major scale

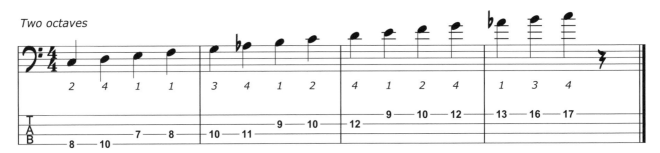

Two octaves

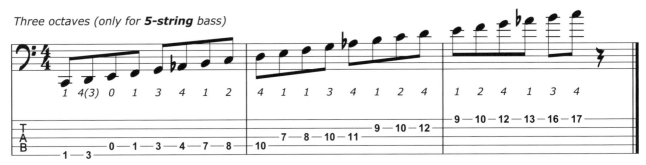

*Three octaves (only for **5-string** bass)*

Chords in relation

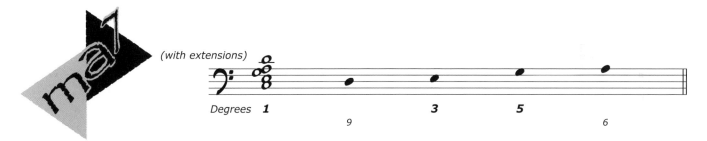

(with extensions)

Degrees **1**   **3**   **5**

9   6

major pentatonic scale

Fingers   2   4   1   4   1   4

Two octaves

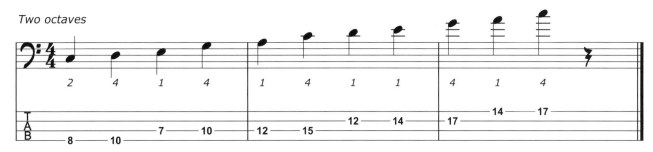

2   4   1   4   1   4   1   1   4   1   4

*Three octaves (only for **5-string** bass)*

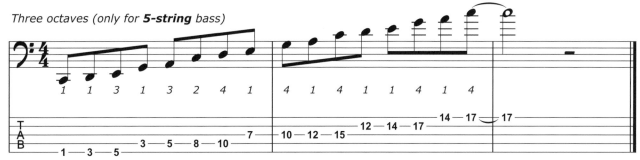

1   1   3   1   3   2   4   1   4   1   4   1   1   4   1   4

Chords in relation

C   C⁶   Cma⁷

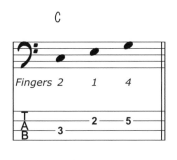   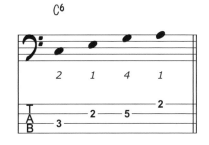   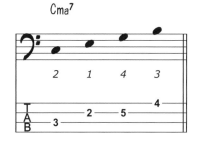

C(add **9**)   C⁶/⁹

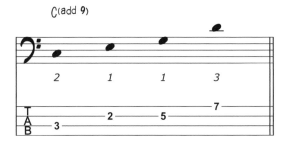   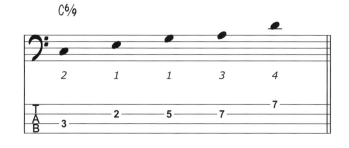

Relationships

mixolydian mode

lydian dominant mode

mixolydian ♭6 mode

mixolydian ♭2 ♭6 mode

diminished h/w scale

blues scale

major pentatonic scale

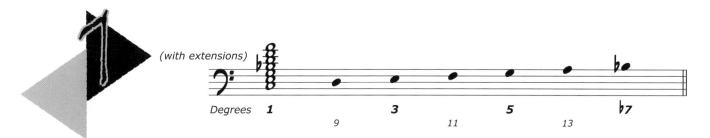

(with extensions)

Degrees **1**   9   **3**   *11*   **5**   *13*   **♭7**

mixolydian mode

Fingers   2   4   1   2   4   1   2   4

Two octaves

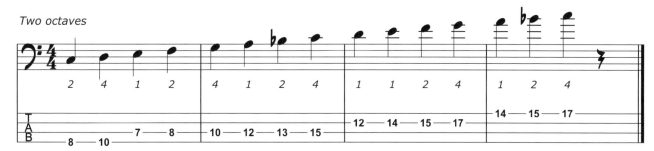

*Three octaves (only for **5-string** bass)*

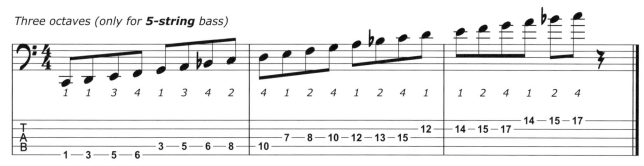

Chords in relation

C

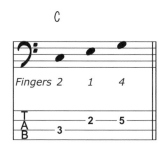

Fingers 2   1   4

C⁷

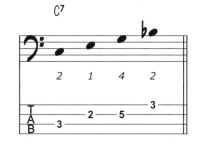

C⁹

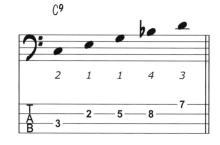

C¹¹

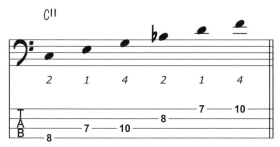

C¹³

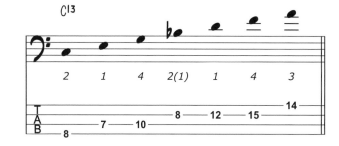

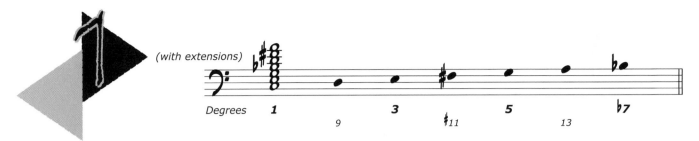

(with extensions)

Degrees   **1**   9   **3**   #11   **5**   13   ♭**7**

lydian dominant mode

Fingers   2   4   1   3   4   1   2   4

Two octaves

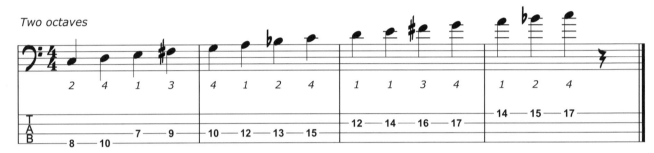

*Three octaves (only for **5-string** bass)*

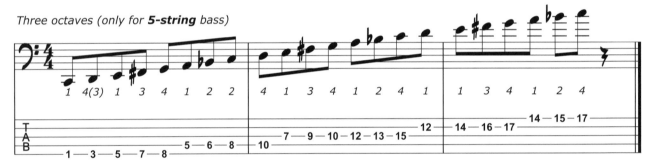

Chords in relation

C   C7   C9

Fingers 2   1   4

C9(#11)   C13(#11)

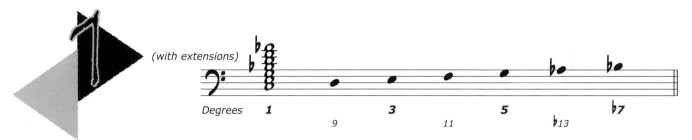

(with extensions)

Degrees	**1**		**3**		**5**		**♭7**
		9		11		♭13	

mixolydian ♭6 mode

Fingers 2   4   1   1   3   4   1   3

Two octaves

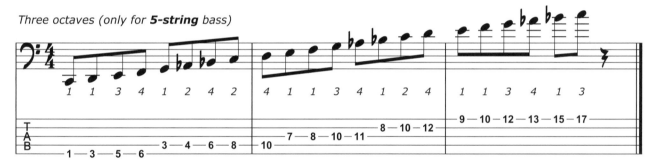

2 4 1 1   3 4 1 2   4 1 1 3   4 1 3

Three octaves *(only for **5-string** bass)*

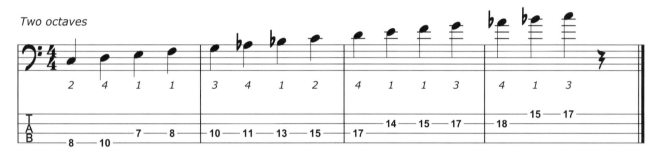

1 1 3 4 1 2 4 2   4 1 1 3 4 1 2 4   1 1 3 4 1 3

Chords in relation

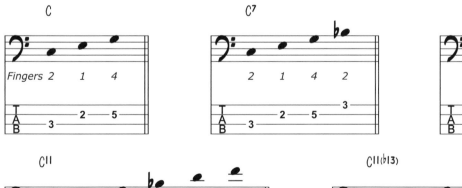

C

Fingers 2   1   4

C7

2   1   4   2

C9

2   1   1   4   3

C11

2   1   4   2   1   4

C11(♭13)

2   1   4   2   1   1   4

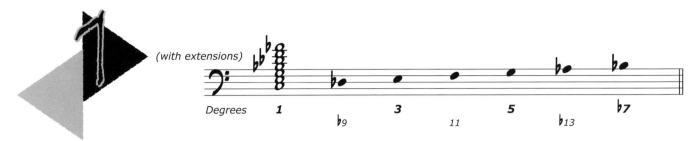

(with extensions)

Degrees **1**   **3**   **5**   **♭7**

♭9   11   ♭13

mixolydian ♭2 ♭6 mode

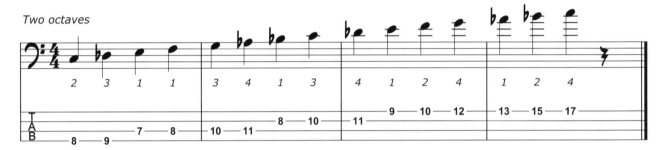

Fingers 2   3   1   1   3   4   1   3

Two octaves

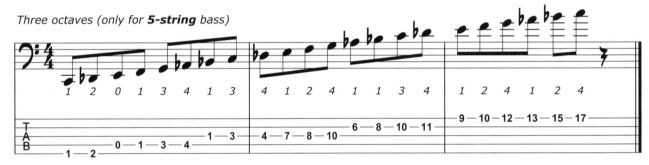

2   3   1   1   3   4   1   3   4   1   2   4   1   2   4

Three octaves (only for **5-string** bass)

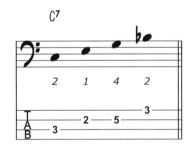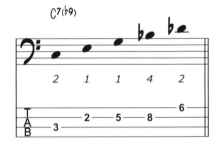

1   2   0   1   3   4   1   3   4   1   2   4   1   1   3   4   1   2   4   1   2   4

Chords in relation

C

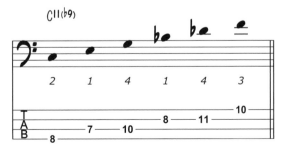

Fingers 2   1   4

C7

2   1   4   2

C7(♭9)

2   1   1   4   2

C11(♭9)

2   1   4   1   4   3

C11(♭9 ♭13)

2   1   1   4   2   1   4

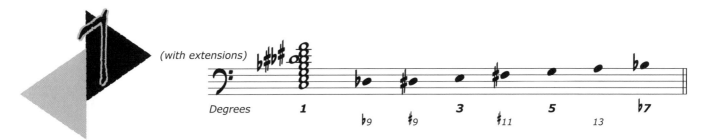

(with extensions)

Degrees   **1**   **3**   **5**   **b7**

b9   #9   #11   13

diminished h/w scale

Fingers 3   4   1   1   3   4   1   2   4

Two octaves

*Three octaves (only for **5-string** bass)*

Chords in relation

C   C7   C7(b9)

Fingers 2 1 4

C7(#9 #11)   C13(b9 #11)

Degrees   **1**   b**3**   (11)   #11   **5**   b**7**

(with extensions)

blues scale

Two octaves

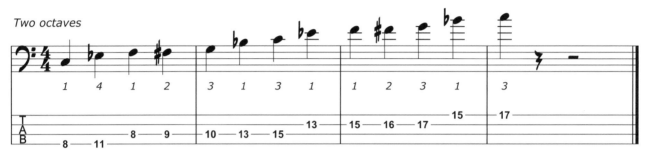

Three octaves (only for **5-string** bass)

Chords in relation

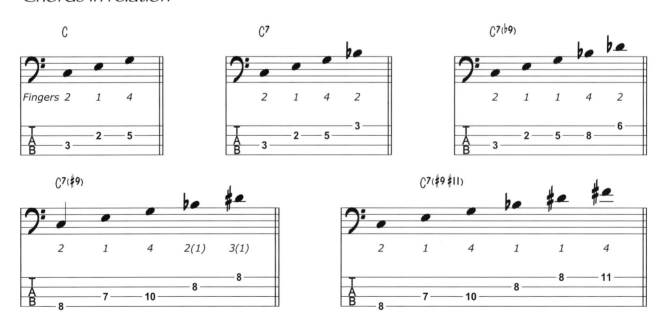

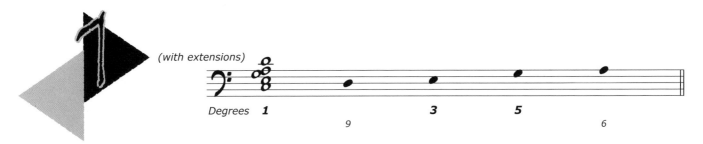

(with extensions)

Degrees   **1**   9   **3**   **5**   6

major pentatonic scale

Two octaves

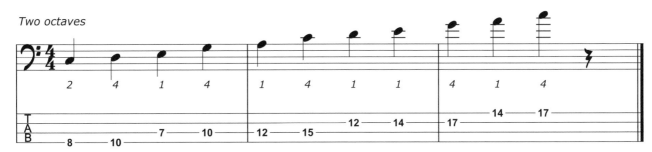

*Three octaves (only for **5-string** bass)*

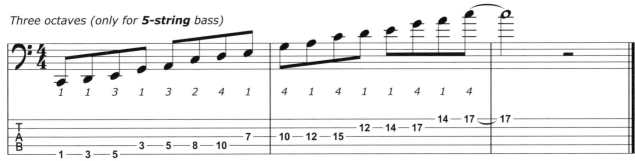

Chords in relation

C

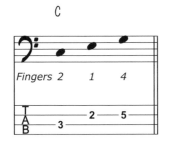

Fingers 2   1   4

C7

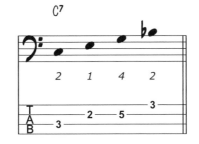

C9

C11 / C13

dorian mode

1   2   b3   4   5   6   b7   8

phrygian mode

1   b2   b3   4   5   b6   b7   8

natural minor scale

1   2   b3   4   5   b6   b7   8

dorian b2 mode

1   b2   b3   4   5   6   b7   8

dorian ♯4 mode

1   2   b3   ♯4   5   6   b7   8

blues scale

1   b3   4   ♯4   5   b7   8

minor pentatonic scale

1   b3   4   5   b7   8

(with extensions)

Degrees **1**   **♭3**   **5**   **♭7**

9   11   13

dorian mode

Two octaves

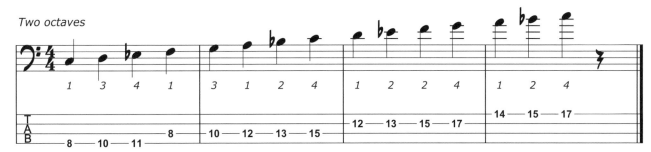

*Three octaves (only for **5-string** bass)*

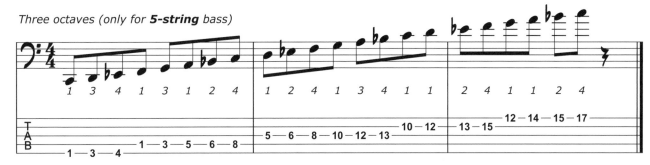

Chords in relation

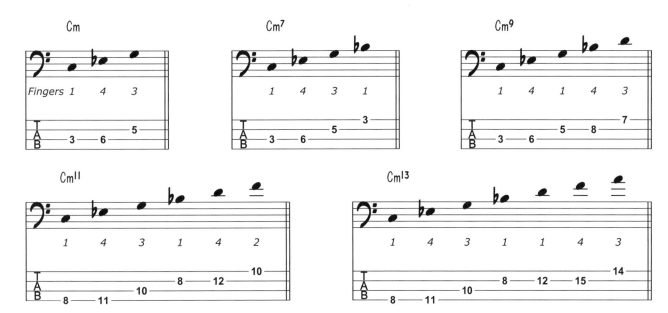

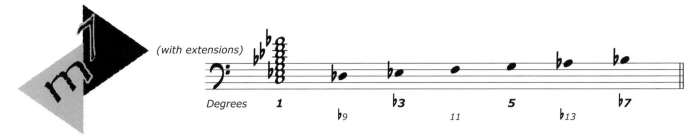

m7 (with extensions)

| Degrees | **1** | ♭9 | **♭3** | 11 | **5** | ♭13 | **♭7** |

phrygian mode

Fingers: 1   2   4   1   3   4   1   3

Two octaves

*Three octaves (only for **5-string** bass)*

Chords in relation

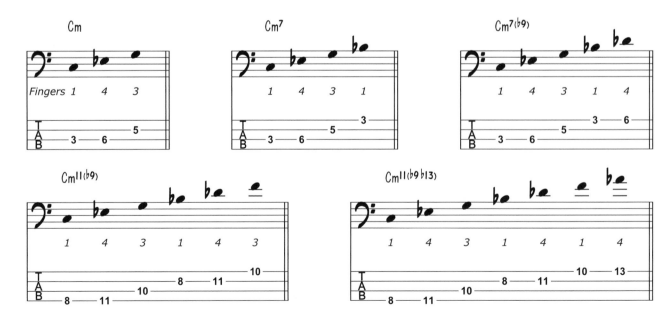

Cm   Cm⁷   Cm⁷⁽♭9⁾

Cm¹¹⁽♭9⁾   Cm¹¹⁽♭9 ♭13⁾

m7 (with extensions)

Degrees **1** | 9 | **b3** | 11 | **5** | b13 | **b7**

natural minor scale

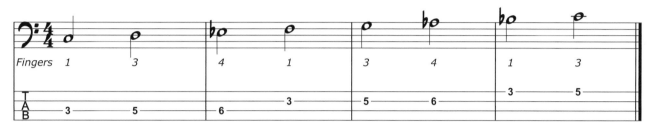

Fingers 1 3 4 1 3 4 1 3

Two octaves

1 1 2 4 1 2 4 1 3 4 1 3 4 1 3

Three octaves (only for **5-string** bass)

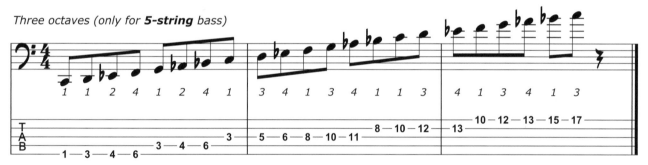

1 1 2 4 1 2 4 1 3 4 1 3 4 1 1 3 4 1 3 4 1 3

Chords in relation

Cm

Fingers 1 4 3

Cm7

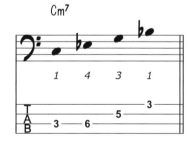

1 4 3 1

Cm9

1 4 1 4 3

Cm11

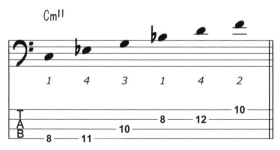

1 4 3 1 4 2

Cm11(b13)

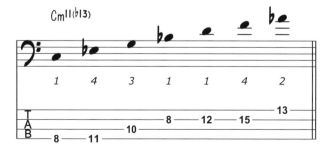

1 4 3 1 1 4 2

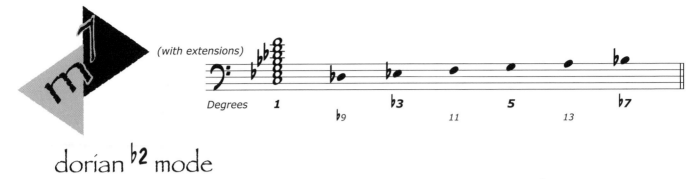

Degrees **1**   ♭9   ♭**3**   11   **5**   13   ♭**7**

dorian ♭2 mode

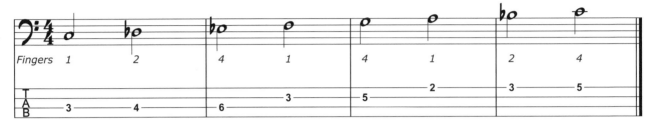

Fingers 1   2   4   1   4   1   2   4

Two octaves

1 2 4 1   1 3 4 1   2 4 1 4   1 2 4

Three octaves (only for **5-string** bass)

1 2 4 1 1 3 4 1   2 4 1 1 3 4 1 2   4 1 3 1 2 4

Chords in relation

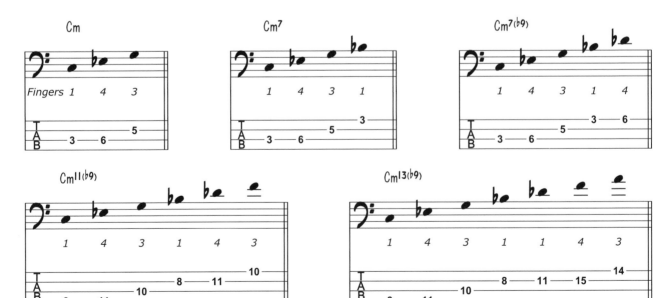

Cm

Fingers 1   4   3

Cm⁷

1   4   3   1

Cm⁷⁽♭⁹⁾

1   4   3   1   4

Cm¹¹⁽♭⁹⁾

1   4   3   1   4   3

Cm¹³⁽♭⁹⁾

1   4   3   1   1   4   3

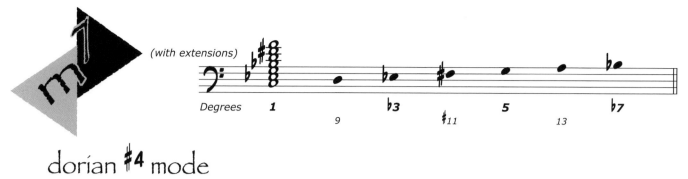

m7 (with extensions)

Degrees **1**   **b3**   **5**   **b7**
   9   #11   13

dorian #4 mode

Fingers   1   3   4   1   2   4   1   3

Two octaves

*Three octaves (only for **5-string** bass)*

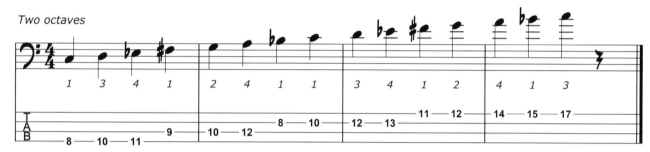

Chords in relation

Cm   Cm7   Cm9

Cm9(#11)   Cm13(#11)

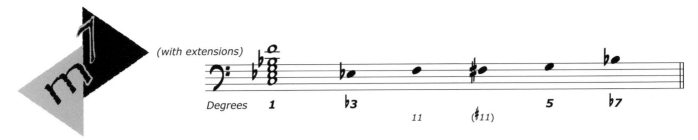

(with extensions)

Degrees   **1**   **♭3**   *11*   *(♯11)*   **5**   **♭7**

blues scale

Fingers   1   4   1   2   3   1   3

Two octaves

*Three octaves (only for **5-string** bass)*

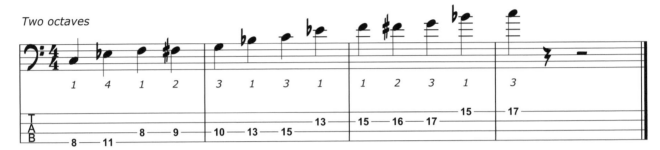

Chords in relation

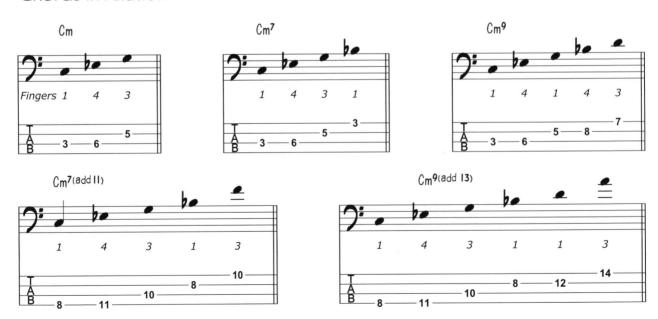

Cm   Cm⁷   Cm⁹

Cm⁷(add 11)   Cm⁹(add 13)

(with extensions)

Degrees **1**   **b3**   **5**   **b7**

11

minor pentatonic scale

Fingers   1   4   1   3   1   3

Two octaves

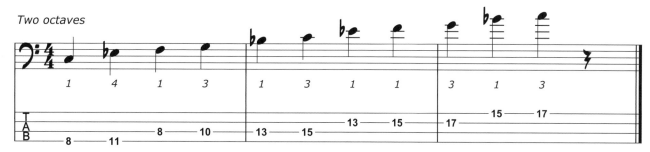

Three octaves (only for 5-string bass)

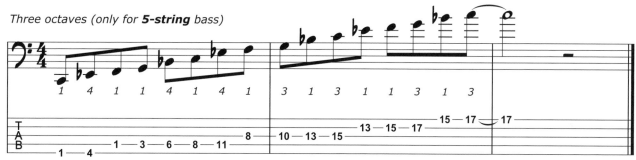

Chords in relation

Cm

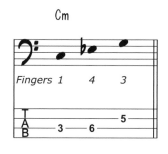

Fingers 1   4   3

Cm7

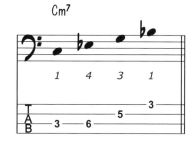

Cm9

Cm11

Cm13

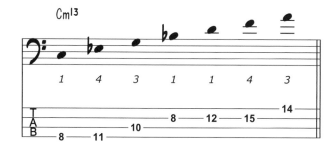

melodic minor scale

1 2 b3 4 5 6 7 8

harmonic minor scale

1 2 b3 4 5 b6 7 8

harmonic major – mode 4

1 2 b3 #4 5 6 7 8

Degrees **1**   9   **♭3**   11   **5**   13   **7**

melodic minor scale

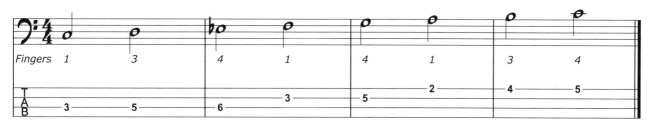

Fingers 1   3   4   1   4   1   3   4

Two octaves

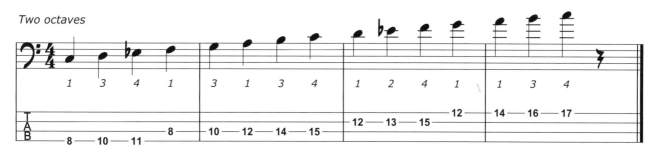

1   3   4   1   3   1   3   4   1   2   4   1   1   3   4

Three octaves (only for **5-string** bass)

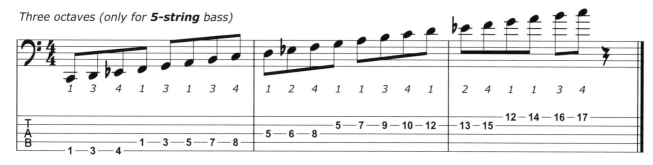

1   3   4   1   3   1   3   4   1   2   4   1   1   3   4   1   2   4   1   1   3   4

Chords in relation

Cm

Cm(ma7)

Cm(ma9)

Fingers 1   4   3

1   4   3   2

1   4   2   1   4

Cm(ma11)

Cm(ma13)

1   4   2   1   4   2

1   4   2   1   1   4   3

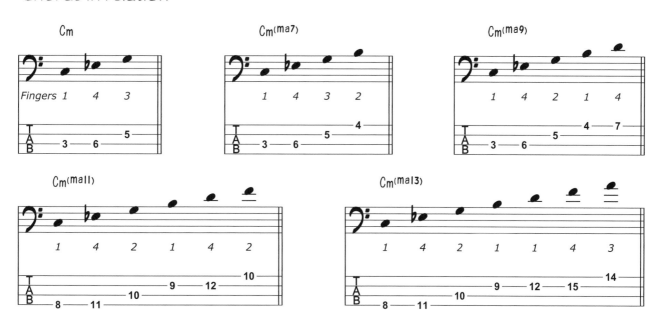

Degrees **1**   9   **♭3**   11   **5**   ♭13   **7**

harmonic minor scale

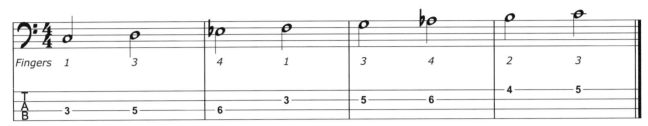

Fingers   1   3   4   1   3   4   2   3

Two octaves

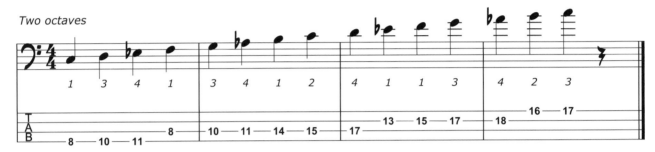

*Three octaves (only for **5-string** bass)*

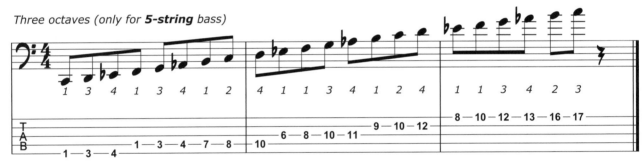

Chords in relation

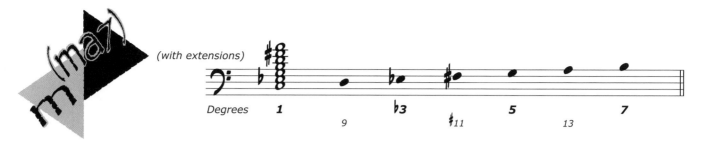

(with extensions)

Degrees **1** **♭3** **5** **7**
9 ♯11 13

harmonic major ~ mode 4

Chords in relation

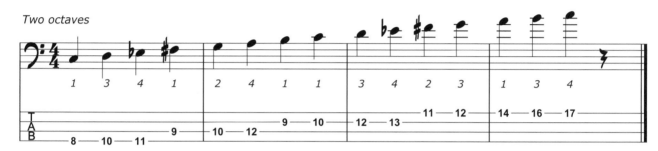

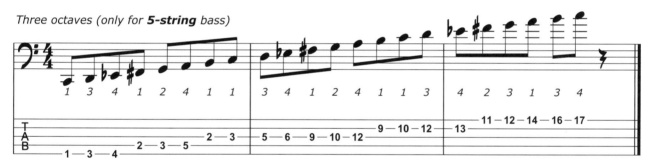

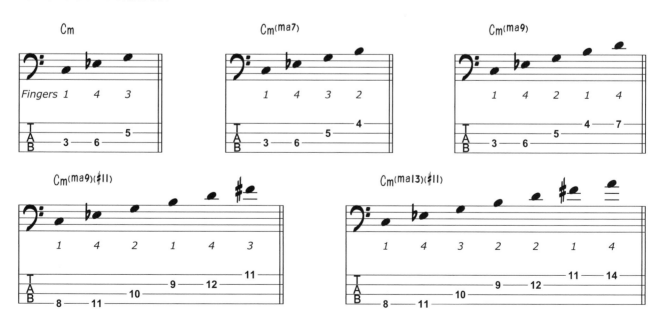

locrian mode

| 1 | b2 | b3 | 4 | b5 | b6 | b7 | 8 |

locrian ♮2 mode

| 1 | 2 | b3 | 4 | b5 | b6 | b7 | 8 |

locrian ♮6 mode

| 1 | b2 | b3 | 4 | b5 | 6 | b7 | 8 |

m7(♭5)

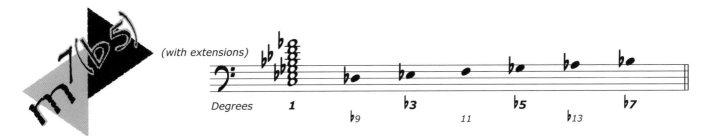

(with extensions)

Degrees: **1** ♭9 **♭3** 11 **♭5** ♭13 **♭7**

locrian mode

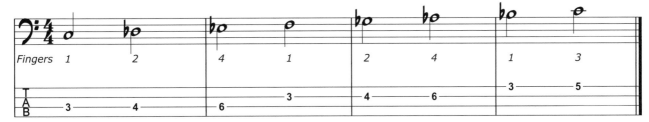

Fingers: 1 2 4 1 2 4 1 3

Two octaves

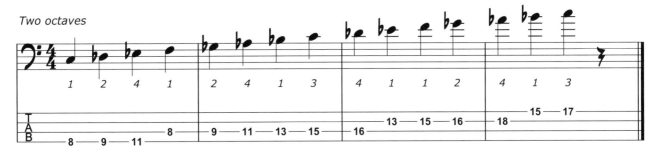

*Three octaves (only for **5-string** bass)*

Chords in relation

C° Cm7(♭5) Cm7(♭5♭9)

Cm11(♭5♭9) Cm11(♭5♭9♭13)

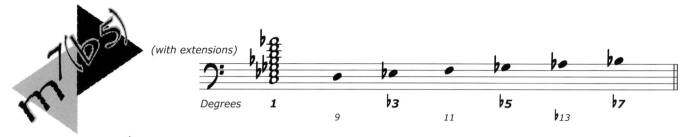

Degrees **1**   b3   b5   b7
9   11   b13

locrian ♮2 mode

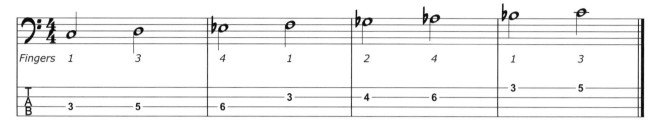

Two octaves

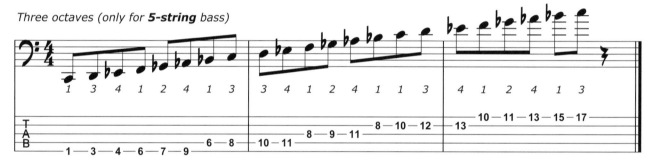

*Three octaves (only for **5-string** bass)*

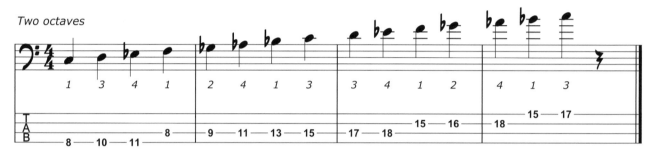

Chords in relation

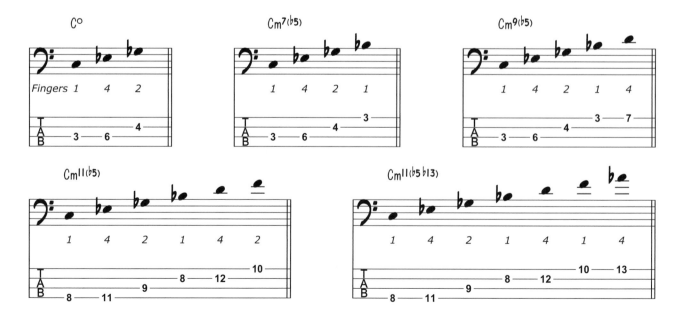

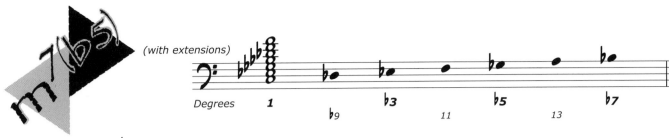

Degrees	1		b3		b5		b7
		b9		11		13	

locrian ♮6 mode

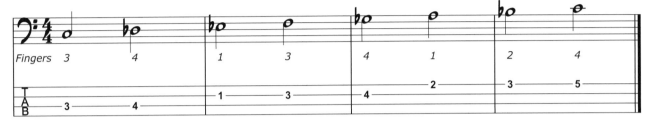

Fingers   3   4   1   3   4   1   2   4

Two octaves

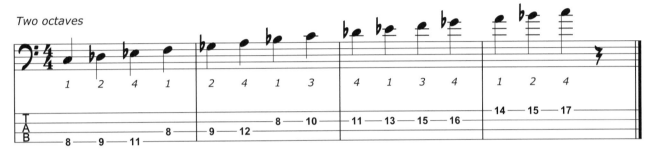

1   2   4   1   2   4   1   3   4   1   3   4   1   2   4

*Three octaves (only for **5-string** bass)*

1 2 4 1 2 0 1 1   2 4 1 2 4 1 3 4   1 3 4 1 2 4

Chords in relation

C°

Fingers 1   4   2

Cm⁷⁽ᵇ⁵⁾

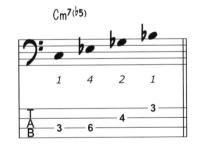

1   4   2   1

Cm⁷⁽ᵇ⁵ᵇ⁹⁾

1   4   2   1   4

Cm11⁽ᵇ⁵ᵇ⁹⁾

1   4   2   1   4   3

Cm13⁽ᵇ⁵ᵇ⁹⁾

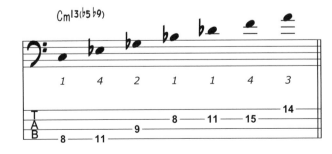

1   4   2   1   1   4   3

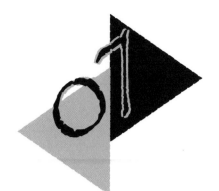

Relationships

diminished scale

1　2　♭3　4　♭5　♭6　♭♭7　♮7　8

altered ♭♭7 mode

1　♭2　♭3　♭4　♭5　♭6　♭♭7　8

harmonic major – mode 7

1　♭2　♭3　4　♭5　♭6　♭♭7　8

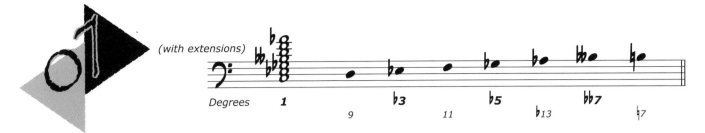

(with extensions)

| Degrees | **1** | 9 | ♭3 | 11 | ♭5 | ♭13 | ♭♭7 | ♮7 |

diminished scale

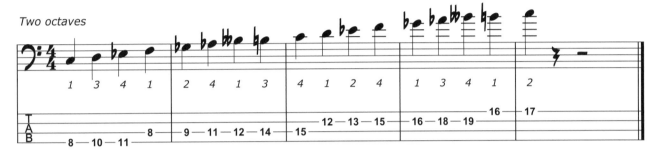

| Fingers | 1 | 3 | 4 | 1 | 1 | 3 | 4 | 1 | 2 |

Two octaves

| 1 | 3 | 4 | 1 | 2 | 4 | 1 | 3 | 4 | 1 | 2 | 4 | 1 | 3 | 4 | 1 | 2 |

*Three octaves (only for **5-string** bass)*

| 1 | 3 | 4 | 1 | 2 | 4 | 1 | 3 | 4 | 1 | 1 | 3 | 4 | 1 | 2 | 4 | 1 | 3 | 4 | 1 | 2 | 4 | 1 | 3 | 4 |

Chords in relation

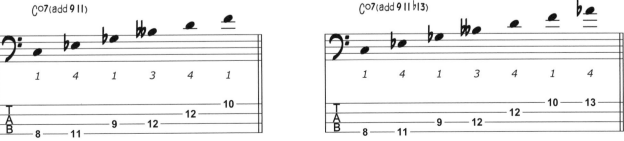

C°

| Fingers | 1 | 4 | 2 |

C°7

| 1 | 4 | 1 | 4 |

C°7(add ma7)

| 1 | 4 | 1 | 4 | 1 |

C°7(add 9 11)

| 1 | 4 | 1 | 3 | 4 | 1 |

C°7(add 9 11 ♭13)

| 1 | 4 | 1 | 3 | 4 | 1 | 4 |

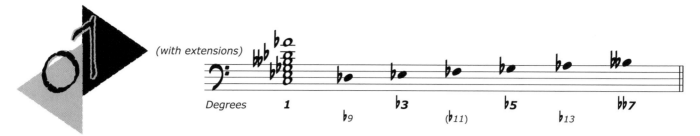

Degrees **1** $\flat$9 $\flat$**3** ($\flat$11) $\flat$**5** $\flat$13 $\flat\flat$**7**

altered $^{\flat\flat 7}$ mode

Fingers 1 1 3 4 1 3 4 2

Two octaves

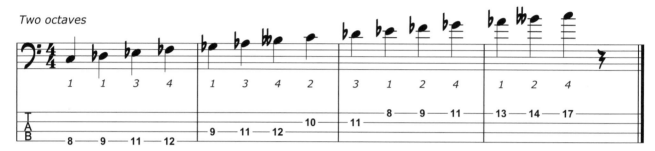

1 1 3 4 1 3 4 2 3 1 2 4 1 2 4

*Three octaves (only for **5-string** bass)*

1 1 3 4 1 3 4 1 1 3 4 1 3 4 2 3 1 2 4 1 2 4

Chords in relation

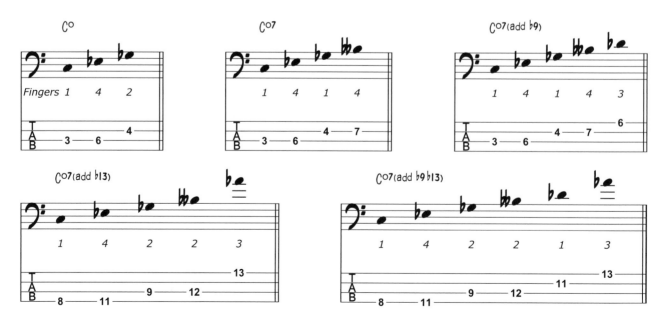

C^{o}

Fingers 1 4 2

C^{o7}

1 4 1 4

C^{o7}(add $\flat$9)

1 4 1 4 3

C^{o7}(add $\flat$13)

1 4 2 2 3

C^{o7}(add $\flat$9$\flat$13)

1 4 2 2 1 3

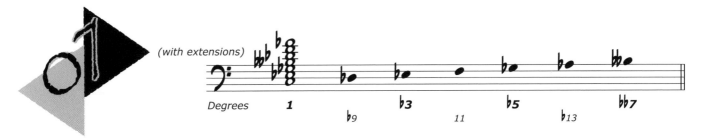

Degrees **1** ♭9 **♭3** 11 **♭5** ♭13 **♭♭7**

harmonic major – mode 7

Fingers 1 2 4 1 1 3 4 2

Two octaves

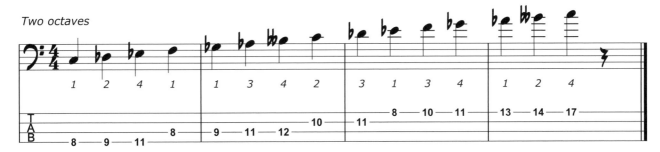

1 2 4 1 1 3 4 2 3 1 3 4 1 2 4

Three octaves (only for 5-string bass)

1 2 4 1 1 3 4 1 2 4 1 1 3 4 2 3 1 3 4 1 2 4

Chords in relation

C°
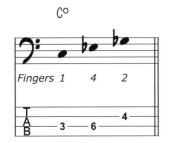
Fingers 1 4 2

C°7

1 4 1 4

C°7(add ♭9)

1 4 1 4 3

C°7(add ♭9 11)

1 4 1 4 3 2

C°7(add ♭9 11 ♭13)

1 4 1 3 2 1 4

augmented scale

lydian augmented mode

ionian ♯5 mode

(with extensions)

Degrees   **1**   #9   **3**   **(5)**   #**5**   **7**

augmented scale

Two octaves

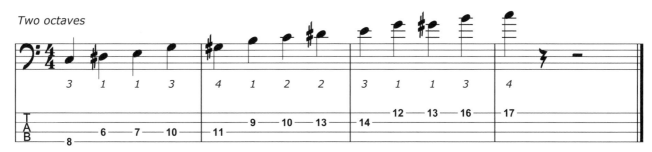

*Three octaves (only for **5-string** bass)*

Chords in relation

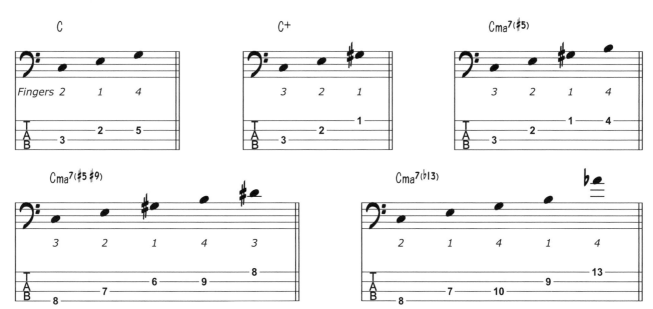

C   C+   Cma⁷(♯5)

Cma⁷(♯5♯9)   Cma⁷(♭13)

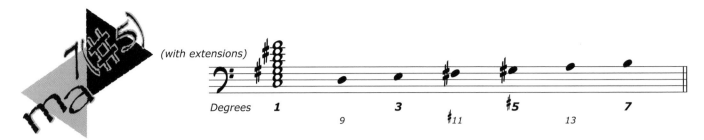

(with extensions)

Degrees **1**   **3**   #**5**   **7**

9   #11   13

lydian augmented mode

Fingers 2   4   1   1   3   4   1   2

Two octaves

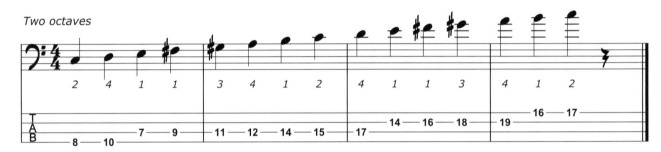

2   4   1   1   3   4   1   2   4   1   1   3   4   1   2

*Three octaves (only for **5-string** bass)*

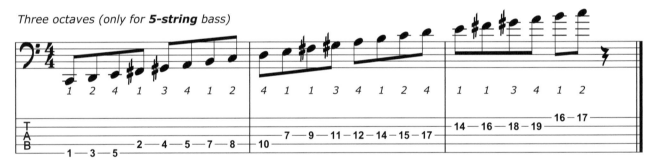

1   2   4   1   3   4   1   2   4   1   1   3   4   1   2   4   1   1   3   4   1   2

Chords in relation

C   Cma⁷⁽♯⁵⁾   Cma⁹⁽♯⁵⁾

Fingers 3   2   1   3   2   1   4   3   2   1   1   4

Cma⁹⁽♯⁵ ♯¹¹⁾   Cma¹³⁽♯⁵ ♯¹¹⁾

3   2   1   1   4   3   2   1   1   4   2   1   4

(with extensions)

Degrees **1**   **3**   **♯5**   **7**

9   11   13

ionian ♯5 mode

Fingers   2   4   1   2   1   1   3   4

Two octaves

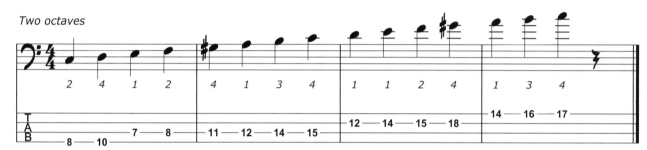

2   4   1   2   4   1   3   4   1   1   2   4   1   3   4

Three octaves (only for **5-string** bass)

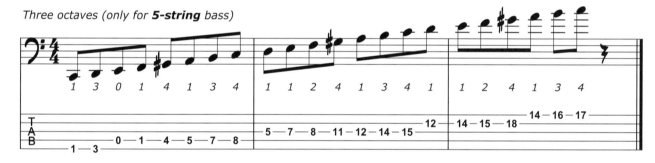

1   3   0   1   4   1   3   4   1   1   2   4   1   3   4   1   1   2   4   1   3   4

Chords in relation

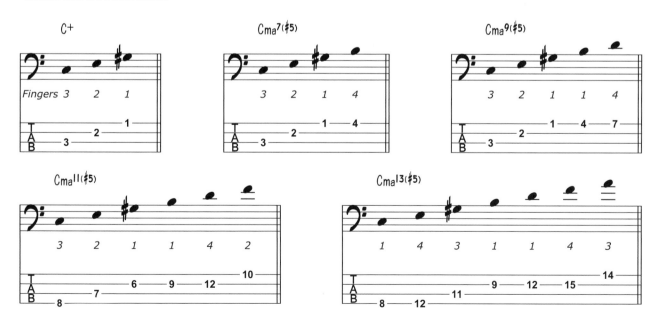

C+

Fingers 3   2   1

Cma⁷⁽♯⁵⁾

3   2   1   4

Cma⁹⁽♯⁵⁾

3   2   1   1   4

Cma¹¹⁽♯⁵⁾

3   2   1   1   4   2

Cma¹³⁽♯⁵⁾

1   4   3   1   1   4   3

7(♯♯5) ——— Chord/Scale

Relationships

whole tone scale

1   2   3   ♯4   ♯5   ♭7   8

altered mode

1   ♭2   ♭3   ♭4   ♭5   ♭6   ♭7   8

major locrian scale

1   2   3   4   ♭5   ♭6   ♭7   8

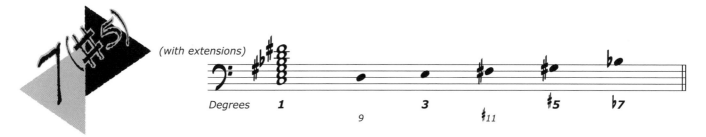

7(#5) *(with extensions)*

Degrees **1** **3** #5 b7
9 #11

whole tone scale

Fingers   1   2   4   1   4   1   3

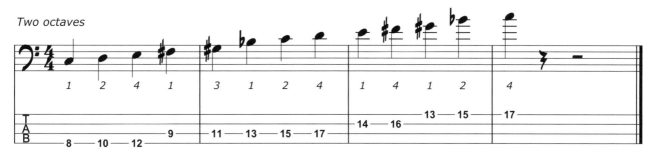

Two octaves

1   2   4   1   3   1   2   4   1   4   1   2   4

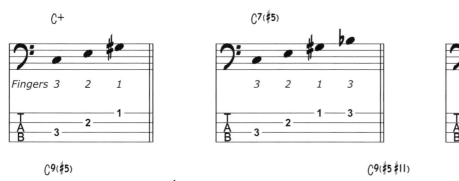

*Three octaves (only for **5-string** bass)*

1   2   4   1   3   1   2   4   1   4   1   1   2   4   1   3   1   2   4

Chords in relation

C+

Fingers 3   2   1

C7(#5)

3   2   1   3

C7(#5)(add #11)

3   2   1   1   4

C9(#5)

3   2   1   3   2

C9(#5 #11)

3   2   1   3   1   4

7(♯5) (with extensions)

Degrees: 1   ♭9   ♯9   3 (♭4)   ♭5   ♯5 (♭6)   ♭7

altered mode

Fingers: 1   1   3   4   1   4   1   3

Two octaves

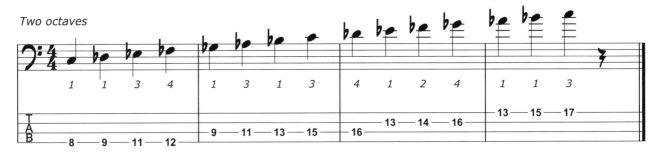

*Three octaves (only for **5-string** bass)*

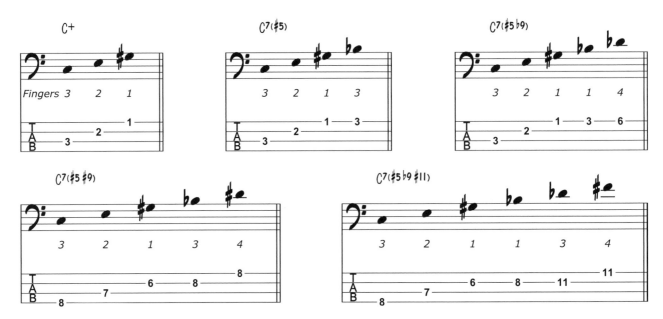

Chords in relation

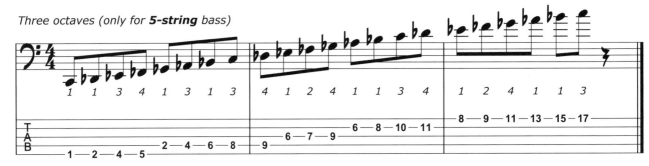

C+

Fingers 3   2   1

C7(♯5)

3   2   1   3

C7(♯5♭9)

3   2   1   1   4

C7(♯5♯9)

3   2   1   3   4

C7(♯5♭9♯11)

3   2   1   1   3   4

 *(with extensions)*

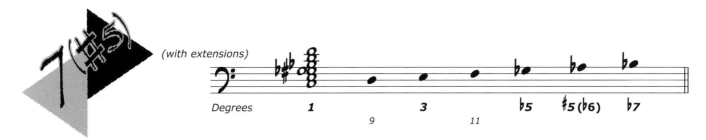

Degrees	**1**		**3**		**b5**	**#5 (b6)**	**b7**
		9		*11*			

major locrian scale

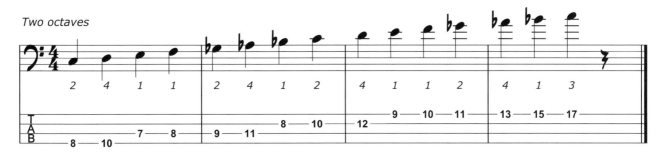

Fingers 2   4   1   1   2   4   1   3

Two octaves

*Three octaves (only for **5-string** bass)*

Chords in relation

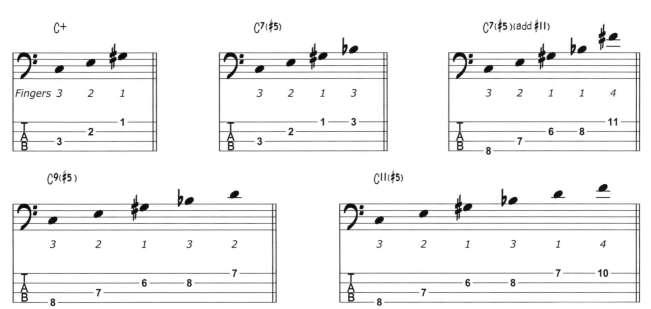

whole tone scale

1   2   3   b5   b6   b7   8

altered mode

1   b2   b3   b4   b5   b6   b7   8

major locrian scale

1   2   3   4   b5   b6   b7   8

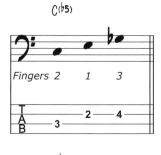 **7(♭5)** *(with extensions)*

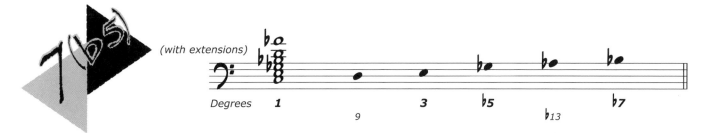

Degrees	**1**		**3**	**♭5**		**♭7**
		9			*♭13*	

whole tone scale

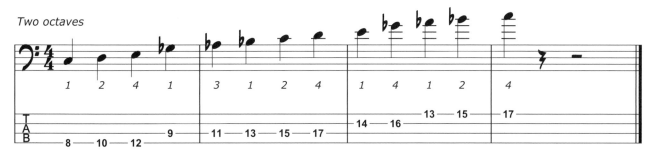

Two octaves

*Three octaves (only for **5-string** bass)*

Chords in relation

C(♭5)

C7(♭5)

C7(♭5)(add♭13)

C9(♭5)

C9(♭5)(add♭13)

7(♭5) (with extensions)

altered mode

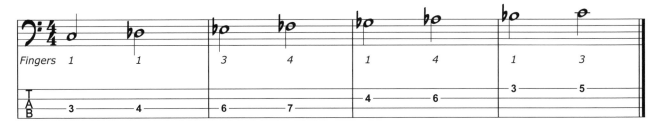

Two octaves

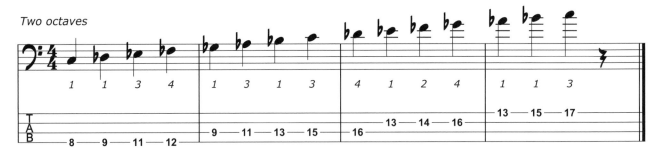

Three octaves (only for **5-string** bass)

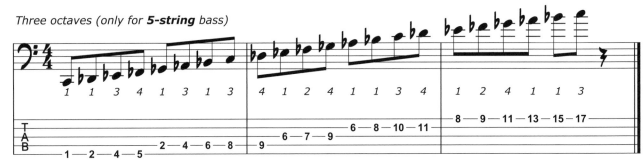

Chords in relation

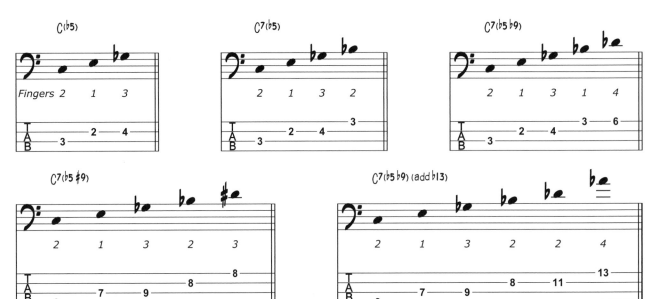

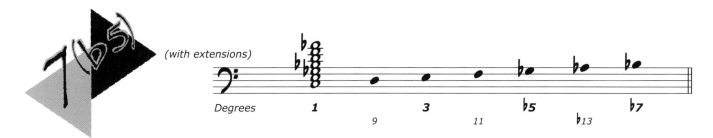

7(♭5) (with extensions)

Degrees	1	3		♭5	♭7
	9	11		♭13	

major locrian scale

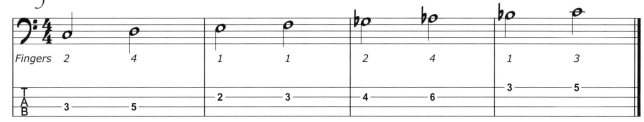

Fingers 2 4 1 1 2 4 1 3

Two octaves

2 4 1 1 2 4 1 2 4 1 1 2 4 1 3

*Three octaves (only for **5-string** bass)*

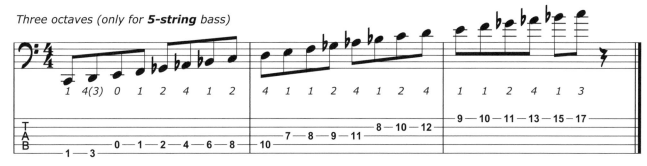

1 4(3) 0 1 2 4 1 2 4 1 1 2 4 1 2 4 1 1 2 4 1 3

Chords in relation

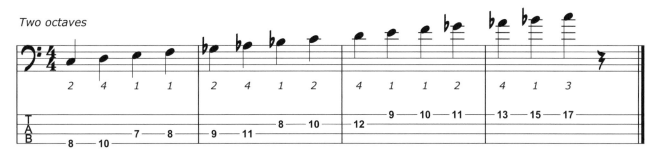

C(♭5)

Fingers 2 1 3

C7(♭5)

2 1 3 2

C7(♭5)(add♭13)

2 1 3 1 3

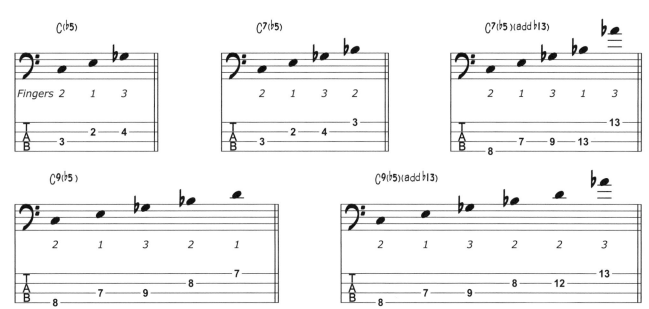

C9(♭5)

2 1 3 2 1

C9(♭5)(add♭13)

2 1 3 2 2 3

Relationships

7sus4

mixolydian mode (no3)

1   2   4   5   6   ♭7   8

major pentatonic - mode 2

1   2   4   5   ♭7   8

kumoi pentatonic - mode 2

1   ♭2   4   5   ♭7   8

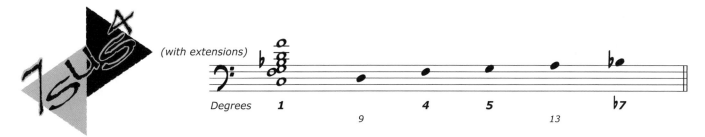

7sus4 *(with extensions)*

Degrees **1** **4** **5** **♭7**

9 13

mixolydian mode (no3)

Fingers 2 4 2 4 1 2 4

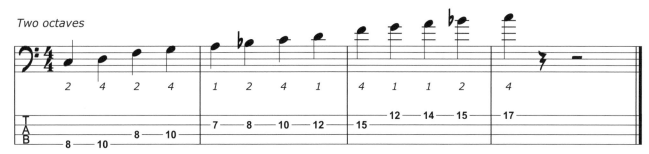

Two octaves

2 4 2 4 1 2 4 1 4 1 1 2 4

Three octaves (only for **5-string** bass)

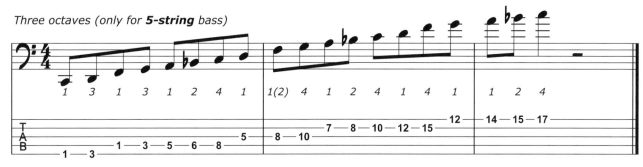

1 3 1 3 1 2 4 1 1(2) 4 1 2 4 1 4 1 1 2 4

Chords in relation

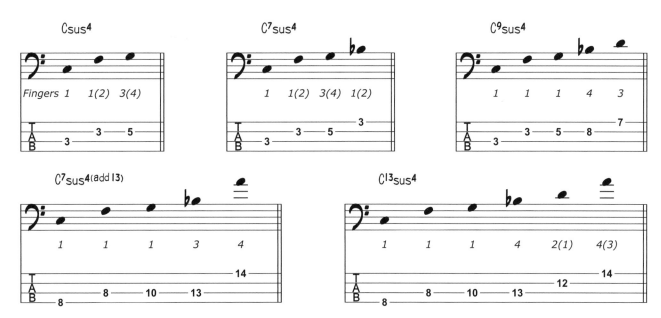

Csus⁴

Fingers 1 1(2) 3(4)

C⁷sus⁴

1 1(2) 3(4) 1(2)

C⁹sus⁴

1 1 1 4 3

C⁷sus⁴(add 13)

1 1 1 3 4

C¹³sus⁴

1 1 1 4 2(1) 4(3)

(with extensions)

Degrees   **1**   **4**   **5**   **b7**

9

major pentatonic - mode 2

Fingers   1   3   1   3   1   3

Two octaves

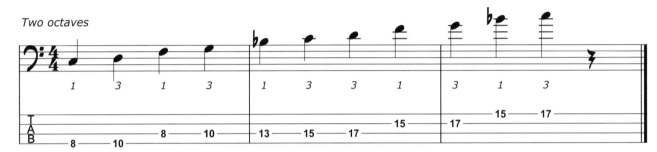

1   3   1   3   1   3   3   1   3   1   3

Three octaves (only for **5-string** bass)

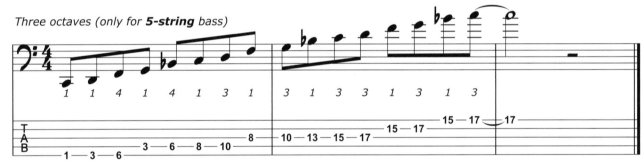

1   1   4   1   4   1   3   1   3   1   3   3   1   3   1   3

Chords in relation

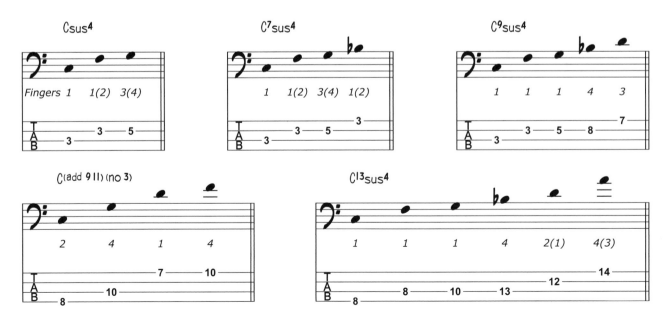

C sus⁴

Fingers 1   1(2)   3(4)

C⁷sus⁴

1   1(2)   3(4)   1(2)

C⁹sus⁴

1   1   1   4   3

C(add 9 11) (no 3)

2   4   1   4

C¹³sus⁴

1   1   1   4   2(1)   4(3)

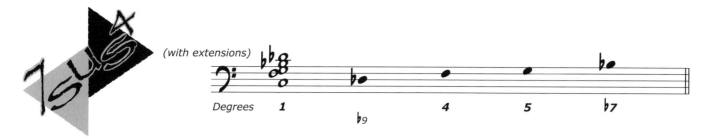

(with extensions)

Degrees   **1**   ♭9   **4**   **5**   ♭**7**

kumoi pentatonic - mode 2

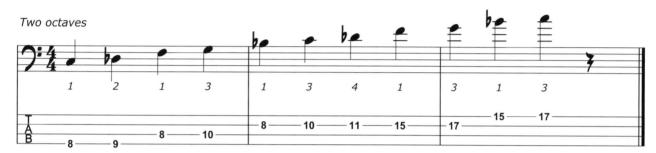

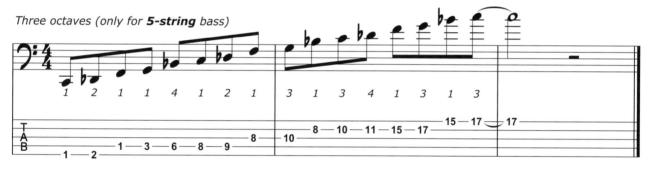

Chords in relation

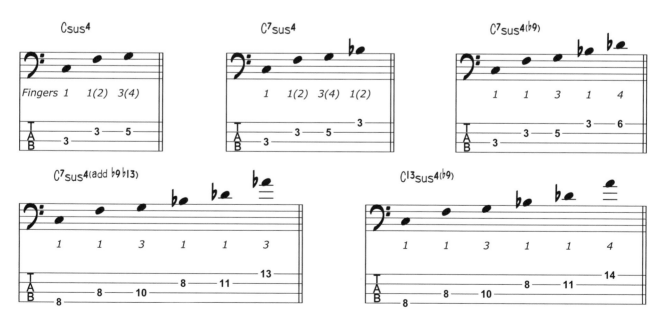

More Great Bass Books from Centerstream...

5-STRING BASS METHOD
by Brian Emmel
Besides discussing how to adapt to the differences in the 5-string versus 4-, this book explores the various ways of using the 5-string, practice tips, different techniques, and practical applications for various genres demonstrated through songs on the 37-minute accompanying CD.
00000134 Book/CD Pack $17.95

ART OF THE SLAP
by Brian Emmel
This slap bass method book, designed for advanced beginning to intermediate bassists, is based on the understanding and application of modes. The focus is on the concept of groove sculpting from modes, and not on actual right- and left-hand techniques. The CD features recordings of all the examples, plus a split-channel option to let you practice your playing. Includes 13 songs.
00000229 Book/CD Pack..$16.95

BASS GUITAR CHORDS
by Ron Middlebrook
84 of the most popular chords for bass guitar. Covers: finger placement, note construction, chromatic charts, and the most commonly used bass scales. Also has a helpful explanation of the common 2-5-1 progression, and the chords in all keys.
00000073 ....$2.95

BEGINNING TO ADVANCED 4-STRING BASS
by Brian Emmel
This instructional video by noted instructor/author Brian Emmel leaves no stone unturned in explaining all there is to know about 4-string bass basics! Designed for the beginning to advanced player, Brian's step-by-step demonstrations form the foundation for understanding music theory and building bass technique. Topics covered range from common musical terminology, to playing in a garage band, to laying down tracks in a recording studio. 60 minutes.
00000374 DVD $19.95

BLUES GROOVES
Traditional Concepts for Playing 4 & 5 String Blues Bass
by Brian Emmel
This book/CD pack has been designed to educate bass enthusiasts about the development of different styles and traditions throughout the history of the blues, from the 1920s to the early 1970s. Players will learn blues scales, rhythm variations, turnarounds, endings and grooves, and styles such as Chicago blues, jazz, Texas blues, rockabilly, R&B and more. The CD includes 36 helpful example tracks.
00000269 Book/CD Pack $17.95

PURRFECT 4-STRING BASS METHOD
by Brian Emmel
This book will teach students how to sight read and to acquire a musical vocabulary. Includes progressive exercises on rhythm notation, 1st to 4th string studies, enharmonic studies, chords and arpeggios, blues progressions, and chord charts.
00000201 ....$9.95

ULTIMATE BASS EXERCISES
by Max Palermo
Bassist and educator Max Palermo takes you through more than 700 easy, step-by-step exercises for finger building, based on the 24 possible fingering combinations. 158 pages.
00000476 ....$19.95

P.O. Box 17878 - Anaheim Hills, CA 92817
(714) 779-9390   www.centerstream-usa.com